CW00847669

THE WRONG SHADE OF YELLOW

MARGARET ELEANOR LEIGH

ISBN-13: 978-1500476298
ISBN-10:1500476293

Chapter 1: Bag Lady with a Bicycle

I was cycling across Europe in search of Utopia, a place I believed was located somewhere in Greece. When I found it, I would start a new life there. It was my big, fat, Greek midlife crisis. But now I was having a crisis within a crisis. What on earth had I been thinking?

I was middle aged and homeless, soon to be penniless, and really and truly no different from that bag lady sitting on the bench over there. I couldn't jack it in and go home, because I didn't have a home to go to anymore. The bicycle and the tent were now home.

Wherever I found myself on any given night was now home. And that meant, for tonight, Genoa Piazza Principe Railway Station was home.

The train from Ventimiglia to Genoa was going more slowly than I could cycle, and that wasn't very fast. When it wasn't crawling along at snail's pace, it was languishing in sidings, and men in silly Italian railway hats were rushing around shouting and gesticulating.

The men in silly hats weren't doing anything useful that I could see and it was in spite of them, rather than because of them, that the train eventually crept into Genoa Piazza Principe Station. Seven hours late, just past midnight.

I was riding on a train instead of on my bicycle, because I couldn't get out of Italy quickly enough. Technically this was cheating, although, as my maths teacher pointed out all those years ago, the only person I was cheating was myself, especially since I'd have got much further and faster if I *had* cycled.

I heaved the bicycle out of the carriage, and noted with dismay that the platform was nowhere near the station concourse. This meant I'd have to unload the panniers, the handlebar bag and bedroll, and transport them in two trips down the long flight of stairs into the bowels of the station. Then I'd have to return for the bicycle, reload it, wheel it through the underground passage to the corresponding flight of stairs leading upwards, where it would be a case of lather, rinse, repeat.

I couldn't do it. I just couldn't. I was worn out, frazzled, more than slightly concerned about the lateness of the hour, and earlier I'd had a Financial Disaster of such epic proportions it merited the use of capital letters.

Now if I just nipped across those empty railway lines, I'd be on the main station concourse in no time. No-one would know. The platform was empty. The railway was deserted. The temptation was overwhelming. All I had to do was break whichever Italian law it is that said you weren't allowed to wheel your bicycle across the railway lines.

They appeared out of thin air, and there were four of them. It wasn't hard to figure out what the word Polizia on their uniforms meant. And though I didn't speak a word of Italian, it wasn't hard to figure out they didn't approve of people wheeling bicycles across railway lines.

I stood there, humiliated and abject, apologizing in English, and wondering how many years you spent in an Italian prison for crossing the line where you weren't supposed to.

After they'd done shouting, and that took a while, I hurried away with my tail between my legs into the great railway terminal building. I was alone at midnight, in an Italian railway station, and I had nowhere to stay. You could say my day wasn't going very well.

Genoa Piazza Principe railway station was a vast nineteenth century structure built in the neo-classical style, all towering pillared arches, marbled walls and high vaulted ceilings. Against such grandeur I looked and felt like a lonely little ant. An ant with a bicycle.

Due to some unfathomably petty railway regulation, I was not permitted to travel with my bicycle on any of the nice fast trains that would have got me out of the place, and the last of the small regional trains that did allow bicycles had long since departed.

My options had shrunk to three. I could venture into a strange city at midnight in search of affordable accommodation; I could dump the bicycle, and continue my journey without it; or I could spend the night on Genoa station.

I wheeled my encumbrance to the great arched entrance and peered out onto the deserted piazza. There was no bright neon sign saying *cozy, inexpensive accommodation this way*. Instead the empty city looked threatening and sinister. The birthplace of Christopher Columbus was probably neither, but I was too low on Columbus-style initiative to venture forth and find out. There was nothing for it but to bed down for the night on the station.

'Bed down' is a misleading phrase. Genoa Piazza Principe may have been a splendid architectural edifice, but a desirable night's lodging it was not. I had a bicycle loaded up with camping equipment that was neither use nor ornament in this particular situation: I could hardly pitch tent on the station concourse. A bitter wind was whistling through the great arched entrances and there were no comfortable seats. The heated waiting room and cafes were all locked. There was just a single hard bench cunningly divided by armrests, to ensure stranded cyclists and other vagrants did not get a good night's sleep. For spite, they'd even locked the toilets. It was shaping up to be a cold and comfortless night.

4

Had I been a young backpacker in my twenties, this might not have been such a big deal. But I wasn't a young backpacker in my twenties; I was a dignified woman of mature years, and so it was a big deal, because dignified women of mature years don't spend nights on stations with bag ladies.

The bag lady was sitting on the bench to my left. She was well into her eighties and I think she was used to the facilities, because in spite of sitting bolt upright, she managed to doze fitfully through the night. Every now and then she'd wake and totter over to peer at the Departures Board, as if she had somewhere to go and a ticket to ride.

But it was obvious she was waiting for the morning light, rather than a train. Two baggy holdalls overspilling with all her worldly goods gave the game away. I could not begin to imagine what set of unfortunate circumstances had brought her life to such a pass. She could have been my mother. She could have been anybody's mother or grandmother. She could be me soon.

To my right on the bench was a Romanian man with a lean and haggard face. He was a migrant laborer, he said, and waiting for a train to Pisa that was due to depart at 7am. There was an earlier train, but that was the express, and much more expensive. He had been working in Italy for several years now, but the work was occasional and poorly paid. He had a wife and three children back in Romania, but he saw them infrequently, a source of suffering for them all. He was hoping they'd be able to join him soon. I could just imagine them, lean and worn as he, living for the day he might send for them.

In the second watch of the night the old woman woke up briefly, pointed to my bicycle, gave a toothless grin, and said "Bravo!" That was heartening because of the bad patch the bicycle and I were going through.

I was properly fed up with the bicycle. I blamed it for my current plight. It was cramping my style and slowing me down. If I didn't have a bicycle, I could get on a train and be transported speedily through Italy in no time. That's what I'd wanted to do ever since arriving in the country just hours earlier, for I had taken a profound dislike to the place.

If I didn't have a bicycle I wouldn't have to spend the night on Genoa station with a bag lady. I wouldn't have to make my way across Italy on regional trains that kept breaking down, or spend four days cycling across it.

Two things stopped me abandoning the bicycle to an unknown Italian fate. First, in spite of our present difficulties, the bicycle was now the closest thing to a friend I had. We'd grown attached in the early days of the trip. We'd had our honeymoon in Holland, had faced adversity together in Belgium, and we'd survived maniacal drivers in France.

We'd developed a relationship. It happens to people and their bicycles on long-distance cycle tours. I had read of this phenomenon with scorn, convinced it would not happen to me. I would never lose sight of the fact that my bicycle was just an inanimate machine.

But by the time we had travelled through the Netherlands, the bicycle and I had grown quite chummy. It began insidiously, with occasional words like "Don't!" when the chain slipped off. Then occasional words turned into full-blown sentences, and before I knew it, I was warning it not to mess with me, or praising it for getting me up a hill. There would be something disloyal in abandoning it after all that.

Also, if I gave up now, and ended my cycle tour before I'd even got to Greece, I would have come full circle: my life would be nothing more than a depressing round of failed enterprises.

And since it was only once I started cheating that the bicycle turned from friend to foe, and since I wasn't supposed to be cheating in the first place, none of this was the bicycle's fault. I needed to get back on the bike, so to speak.

6

There was a train to Rimini, on the other side of Italy, that was departing Genoa at 7.15am. I'd catch that, I decided, because I'd heard there were Alps in the way and I was keen as mustard to avoid those. But from Rimini I would start using it again; I'd cycle the hundred or so kilometers to Ancona, and from there I would catch the first available ferry to Greece.

Everything would be peachy once I got to Greece. There'd be milk and honey flowing from the hills, and it wouldn't matter nearly so much that now, thanks to the Financial Disaster — and more about that later — there were just weeks instead of months between me and starvation.

In the third watch of the night, the bag lady, the migrant and I were joined by a woman wearing just a towel. She livened things up no end, because the only entertainment before that was the announcement board ticking over, telling of trains I wasn't allowed to catch, and even that ceased around 3am. The woman in the towel hopped about a fair bit, but seemed very happy, a good deal too happy given the conditions. It was freezing on that station even with the benefit of clothing, and I never did find out why she wasn't wearing any.

Every hour the four-strong patrol of railway police with whom I had had the earlier encounter emerged from their cozy heated office and stomped up and down. The first few times I was worried they'd throw us into the night, but they took no notice at all and I suspect this was because we looked like a travelling circus rather than terrorists.

When a welcome cold dawn ended a night that had seemed to last forever, the Romanian man pulled some oranges from a shabby rucksack. He shared them with us, his fellow flotsam of humanity thrown together for a single night on Genoa station.

I had read that Genoa was a spectacular city; it was dubbed "the Superb One" on account of its architecture, art and gastronomy. I couldn't have cared less about any of that. I'd had more than enough of Genoa. I wanted to continue my midlife crisis somewhere else, anywhere else so long as it wasn't Italy.

But Italy wasn't done with me yet. It was a spiteful country, was Italy. I don't understand what people see in it, or why they want to go and live there. Someone told me once that you either love Greece or you love Italy, and that it's simply not possible to love both. Loving both would be a bit like being Catholic and Protestant at the same time. It's just not possible. This was an interesting claim, and one with which I heartily concurred, although I grant that two opinions fall a little short of a full statistical sampling.

This was not my first time in Italy. I'd been there before, in my early twenties. That time I had been travelling in the opposite direction, leaving Greece and heading north for France, and Italy was spiteful even back then. I'd gone to the Post Office to change some traveler's cheques — this was back in the days when that's how travel money worked — and the woman had cheated me. I hadn't checked what she was doing because this was the Post Office, and I trusted her. It wasn't as if she was a dodgy back street money changer, and if you can't trust the Post Office who can you trust? When I realized what had happened it was already too late and my relationship with Italy never recovered. It's not that I'm unforgiving, but nothing ever happened in Italy afterwards to erase that early negative impression.

The ticket office opened at last at 7am. The train to Rimini departed at 7.15. I had just fifteen minutes to explain to the surly ticket seller (who didn't or wouldn't speak English), that I needed a ticket to Rimini for myself and one for my bicycle, for in Italy bicycles are issued with their own train tickets. Aware of my urgency she immediately went on a go-slow, her revenge upon a world that had decreed she be a ticket seller.

By the time she had printed out the tickets, I had just minutes to heave my bike and gear down the three flights of stairs, through the underground passageway and up the other side onto the railway platform, since of course the train for Rimini was on the furthest possible platform, and nipping across the railway lines was now out of the question. I could have caught the next train, departing a few hours later, but I was filled with an irrational and overwhelming desire to escape the scene of my night's lodgings.

In Italy, you don't simply purchase your train ticket and then board the train. That would be too simple. Italian Rail thoughtfully provides little boxes at the entrance to each platform, where you are supposed to insert your ticket — and your bicycle's ticket — for a date stamp, before you board the train.

In the panicky rush of it all, I forgot to date stamp our tickets, the bicycle's and mine, and rushed past the machine without even noticing it. It was an honest, and you would have thought fairly common mistake for a foreigner to make, one that could easily be rectified at the next station, or overwritten in some way or another.

The train conductor, a tiny cartoon caricature of an Italian man, complete with Garibaldi moustache, thought otherwise. He seized my unstamped tickets and rounded on me in a torrent of angry Italian, of which I understood not a word. Then he wrote the sum €35 on a piece of paper and thrust it under my nose, uttering his one word of English, a word he had clearly practiced a lot: "Pay!"

I protested. At first I did not understand what he was shouting about, and then I remembered the little machine that I had neglected in my haste, and it dawned on me that the demand for €35 had something to do with that.

"Pay!" he said again, more loudly this time.

I shook my head. "I'm sorry," I said. "It was a mistake. And no, I am not going to give you €35."

"Pay!" He screamed. And then he screamed it over and over, "Pay! Pay! Pay!"

It is not pleasant when a small, but very scary Italian man sticks his nose two inches from your own and screams "Pay" repeatedly at the top of his voice. Especially after you have just had a terrible night sitting upright on a hard bench on a freezing station. When he saw I was adamant, for in light of the Financial Crisis €35 was an awful lot of money, he revised the asking price.

He scribbled again on his piece of paper. He crossed out the €35 and amended it to €5. This did nothing for his credibility. If there was indeed an official fine for forgetting to stamp your ticket, the sum would surely not be negotiable.

So I shook my head. He really lost it then, and was soon quite literally jumping up and down on the spot, screaming "Pay, Pay, Pay." The other occupants in the carriage looked on with mild interest to see who was going to win the battle.

Eventually when he threatened, by means of gesture (and the gesture, which was unmistakable, was that of throwing the bicycle off the train), I capitulated, and gave him his €5, making it clear what I thought of his tactics, what I thought of him, and what I thought of Italy. And then I burst into tears and cried the rest of the way to Rimini.

The effect of this encounter was to intensify the desire to depart this land of surly ticket sellers and men in railway uniforms who shouted at me. Everything would be better in Greece. No-one would shout at me in Greece.

But there were still 100 kilometers to travel from Rimini to Ancona and the most I had cycled in a day thus far had been sixty. A train would have taken me there in just over an hour, but I was well and truly done with trains. Nothing would have induced me back into another train station and onto another Italian train.

So I spent that night in a little hotel in a village near Rimini, because it was cheaper than the gaudy and overpriced camping ground. Then, grateful for the flatness of the terrain, I set off for Ancona at breakneck speed the next morning, and managed my best day's cycling to date.

The road from Rimini to Ancona confirmed everything I already suspected about Italy: it was the land where everything had a price. On my left was the beach, and I wanted to stop for lunch and sit there for a while, eating my bread and cheese. But no, the beach was carved up and claimed by the endless strip of hotels, restaurants and bars on my right. Each appeared to *own* the piece of beach opposite, with the start of new ownership signaled by a different colored set of deck loungers and umbrellas. If you were a patron or resident at one of those establishments you got to use that particular strip of beach. If you weren't a resident you paid. So either way you paid. Pay! Pay! Pay! It was becoming a familiar refrain.

I hadn't realized that beaches could be anything other than the public property of all, there for all to enjoy, and found something deeply offensive in this arrangement. Next thing, I thought, they'll be trying to sell entry into heaven itself. And then I remembered they'd already done that, back in the middle ages, with the sale of indulgences, and that Martin Luther had taken a similarly dim view of that, his protests so effective the entire history of Western Christianity changed forever.

But at least they didn't carve up and sell the beaches of Greece, and that was a thought that lent wings to feet that were pedaling harder than they'd done before. Perhaps if I made Ancona before the last ferry sailed, I'd not have to spend another night in this terrible country.

But Italy still wasn't done with me. It was 7pm when I arrived, exhausted and desperate, at Ancona's deserted ferry terminal, a vast and confusing place. There was a maze of flyovers all offering different options, none of which made any sense at all. Each road was signposted with an identical picture of a ferry and something unhelpful written beneath. Thus one of the roads led to the "New Ferry," another to the "Tourist Ferry," and yet another to the "Car Ferry."

I had no idea which ferry I needed, but thought Tourist Ferry seemed the most logical. I had overlooked the fact that this was Italy, where the connections with logic were tenuous at best, and the correct ferry terminal for tourists was in fact the Car Ferry.

So, after wasting an hour trying to understand Italian signage and setting off in the wrong direction in search of the Tourist Ferry (which I never found), I finally arrived at the correct terminal. And there, just pulling out of harbor, sailing joyfully in the direction of the promised land, was the last ferry of the day.

The terminal building was still open, but it was empty; everyone else had escaped from Italy, and the next day's sailing schedule was displayed on an electronic board. There were stacks of free brochures outside the booking booths, with pictures of happy passengers, headed for the promised land, sitting around in comfortable lounges and coffee bars, attended by friendly Greek waiters.

The dismay I felt at being stuck in Italy one more night was quite disproportionate to the reality of the situation. What difference would one more night in Italy make? It would only be my third, counting the one on Genoa station. I'd be out of this dreadful country tomorrow.

It was tiredness that was my undoing, I think. I mounted my bicycle, exhausted, trying not to cry, (yes I am a cry-baby), and set off in the direction of the town.

I did not notice the sunken railway tracks embedded in the concrete of the ferry terminal. The front wheel of the bicycle got stuck in one of these and stopped moving. I, unfortunately, did not.

I hit the concrete on my right side with a sickening crunch, unable to move and unable to breathe. I thought I was dying. I thought I was on my way to meet Jesus. I thought I had punctured my lung and that I'd be dead in a matter of minutes.

Somehow, many minutes later and still not dead, I managed to raise myself to a sitting position. The tearing pain in the region of my ribcage intensified a hundredfold. Across the concrete terminal, on the other side of a high wire fence, and across a busy road, a group of Italians sitting at a café table had witnessed my fall and were now all standing up, watching curiously. I managed a feeble thumbs-up and a shouted "I'm okay," and they returned to their coffee.

But I was not okay. It took an eternity to stand up and reload the bicycle. My panniers and handlebar bag were scattered about the concrete. I worried about the fate of my laptop and camera and hoped the padding provided by the surrounding luggage had sufficed as protection.

I wheeled the bicycle slowly back through the maze of exits and flyovers to Ancona's station square, around which were clustered a selection of unappealing, but inexpensive railway hotels. Every movement was agony, so this was no time for shopping around and I took a room in the nearest of them. It was seedy, and there was no ensuite, just a communal bathroom down the passage. Still, it was cleanish, there was a little balcony and the hotelier seemed a decent man for an Italian.

I checked the laptop, and found it had fared better than I. Being one of the first laptops ever manufactured, it had been built to last. I lowered myself gingerly onto the bed and opened a bottle of cheap Italian wine I had bought earlier with which to celebrate the leaving of that country and that had somehow survived the fall. In so doing I discovered just how difficult it is to uncork wine with broken ribs. (I was in no doubt that I had broken at least one of them.) And then I anaesthetized myself against both pain and dark doubts with cheap Italian plonk.

Was my big fat Greek midlife crisis over before it had even properly begun?

Chapter 2: Big Fat Greek Midlife Crisis

Six Months Earlier

I used to do time at the Ministry of Human Misery in New Zealand. Then I had my big fat Greek midlife crisis and everything changed.

The Ministry of Human Misery was not, of course, its real name. It had a proper name like Labour or Education or Taxes, but I had signed a piece of paper swearing me to secrecy. I didn't read it because it was boring, and since I have no idea exactly what it was I agreed to, it is probably wise to err on the side of caution and not say which Ministry it was. Besides, Ministry of Human Misery more accurately conveys what we did there: we made as many people as possible as miserable as possible and got paid for it.

I didn't choose to become a briefing paper advisor there. I was tricked into it by Raymond, a devious civil servant, which is probably a tautology. A temp agency sent me there to fill in for the previous incumbent, who was recovering in a mental hospital somewhere.

As far as I was concerned, the assignment couldn't be temporary enough, and so when Raymond asked me if I'd like to apply for the permanent position, I didn't even have to think about it."I'd rather be boiled in oil and eaten by a tribe of savages."

Raymond smiled and while I didn't understand at first why he did so, all was revealed at morning tea a few weeks later. Morning teas were extravagant affairs, their exorbitant cost hidden under layers of clever accounting and paid for by the tax-payer. A week's morning teas at the Ministry of Human Misery would have released at least one small African nation from the grip of famine.

The thinking behind them was that they pacified the workforce, ensuring we did not, like lemmings, throw ourselves out of the windows. There was perhaps a more effective strategy in place ensuring we did not do this, and that was there were no windows. The Ministry of Human Misery was just a large concrete box, painted hospital green and lit with bilious strips of florescent lighting.

"I have an announcement to make," Raymond said with a smirk, while I shoveled down chocolate éclairs and tried not to think about throwing myself out of a window. "Let's have a big round of applause for Margaret."

That got my attention.

"I am delighted to announce Margaret has been successful in her application for the permanent post of Briefing Paper Advisor," he said and everyone clapped. "Human Resources will be sending the paperwork down later."

Since I could hardly resign from a job five minutes after my appointment, there wasn't a lot I could do about it. It felt like God was having a laugh.

To the uninitiated, the life of a ministerial advisor might even sound quite exciting. I got to rush around with important-looking papers, saying stuff like: "The Minister needs to know what's going on *right now!*"

But the reality was traumatic, rather than exciting. I was caught between two opposing forces with nowhere to run. On one side were the ambitious manager types, people who had got to be managers by sticking the requisite number of knives in the requisite number of backs. They spent all day shouting: "Where the hell is the briefing paper?" or "This briefing paper is crap – send it back and get it rewritten."

On the other side were the producers of briefing papers, pouring forth all their excuses why their papers were late, or why they were crap. No-one ever produced briefing papers on time or of adequate quality because a) everyone hated producing briefing papers; b) they were too busy improving their Free Cell averages; or c) they simply weren't there.

And the reason for c) was that the Ministry of Human Misery had one of the highest rates of absenteeism in the country. This was generally blamed on the building. "It's a sick building," people would say. "There's Legionnaire's disease coming in through the air conditioning."

So epidemic were the outbreaks of this unidentifiable but virulent illness, the powers that be even arranged for health and safety technicians to come out and do tests, but they never did find any hard evidence of Legionnaire's disease. I suspect the cause was more sinister and ultimately less solvable. People got ill all the time because that's what happened when you spent your days making other people miserable.

In sum, it was the worst job I'd ever had. It was even worse than the job in another government department, which I shall call the Department of Nagging, just because I can. There my function was to spend all day on the phone, ringing small business owners and nagging them to return some or other nitpicking form.

These unfortunate business owners had all won the booby prize in a sadistic lottery devised by the government, requiring them to fill in about 20 pages of forms, once a month, for the rest of their lives. Everyone who'd won this lottery hated it, no-one ever bothered filling in their forms, and so the Department was forced to employ full-time Naggers, of whose number I was one for a period of three weeks.

That is about as long as any human being can be expected to last as a government Nagger. After spending a whole day nagging, I would go home completely unable to speak.

The briefing paper advisor role was worse also than the middle-of-the-night job I'd once had cleaning a bakery that was always covered floor to ceiling in sticky icing and jam, and worse than the job where I'd sat at a reception desk, ruling lines in an empty ledger all day. If that doesn't sound too bad, try ruling lines in an empty ledger for just twenty minutes and see what it does to your sanity.

Nevertheless, not everyone at the Ministry hated it there. There were even a few who found the business of making people miserable quite satisfying. These were the lovers of process, folk who found meaning and satisfaction in implementing decisions in a paint-by-numbers fashion.

If the answer to question 7 is no, go to question 12. If the answer is yes, go to question 8. If the answer to that question 8 is no, print out and post rejection letter number 3. If the answer to question 8 is yes, print out and post rejection letter number 11. If the answer is don't know, print out and post rejection letter No. 5.

But for the large majority, of whom I was one, the Ministry of Human Misery was pure purgatory. We all died a little each day. We were the ones who started watching the clock at 9.20 am, after we'd sidled, late again, into our desks, hoping no-one had noticed. (Someone always noticed.) We were the ones who spent as much of each day as possible improving our Free Cell averages, or writing novels on the sly.

Please get me out of here, I said to God, but God didn't seem to be listening.

And then I woke up in the surgical ward of Wellington Hospital. This was not quite what I'd had in mind when I'd said, *Please get me out of here,* but it was certainly effective. The mysterious ability of the building to make people very ill indeed had had its way with me also.

Chapter 3: The Flaws in the Plan

There was a drip attached to my arm feeding six different drugs into my bloodstream. The specialist, with his retinue of trainees, was muttering darkly about surgery and I was in a lot of pain. I had a series of life-threatening ruptures and constrictions running through my intestines.

I dragged myself out of bed, and down the hospital corridor, wheeling my drip-machine beside me, while the hospital gown flapped inadequately about, as hospital gowns tend to do. I found a telephone in the lobby, and made a call to Raymond to tell him I wasn't going to be in that day, or the next day, or the day after.

"Damn," said Raymond. "What am I going to do about the latest briefing paper on increasing the misery of the nation?"

There was no "I'm terribly sorry to hear that. Are you all right? Is there anything we can do?" There was just "So when do you think you will be back to sort it all out?"

How about never? I am in hospital. I am on a drip. I don't even know what day it is because of the six different drugs they are pumping into my bloodstream. And you are telling me about a briefing paper crisis. It is because of briefing paper crises that I am in hospital in the first place.

I didn't say any of it, because I felt too ill, and besides there was little point, because Raymond never listened to a word anyone said anyway. So I shuffled back to my hospital bed, where I began, mentally, to compose a letter of resignation.

This unexpected detour into hospital had been building for a while: the pain, the repressed awareness that something had gone badly wrong with my innards. Then at last, there had been that reluctant visit to a GP that had sealed my fate.

"You are going to hospital," she said reaching for the telephone, "and you are going right now."

So there I was in Wellington hospital, some 25 years away from retirement with only another thousand or so Monday mornings to go, facing the knowledge that if I stayed in the Ministry of Human Misery, there probably wouldn't even be a retirement. I would be dead in a couple of years, a victim of the mysterious illness that eventually got everyone who worked there. As it was, I felt like the living dead.

There was a woman in the bed opposite me. She was in her fifties and she too had been struck down with mysterious Government Department Illness. She was in a terrible state. She'd had some unexpected and catastrophic collapse which meant she could not walk and was not expected to walk ever again. She had bags to take care of bowel and bladder movements and required assistance to turn over in bed. Her helplessness and her frustration were all too apparent. Her only solace was books, and she escaped the reality of her situation in a large pile of murder mystery novels.

What filled me with horror, quite apart from her situation itself, was that she had held a responsible and highly stressful government position before being struck down pretty much overnight. There was surely a connection between her previous occupation and her current plight. In ten years time that might be me. No, in ten years that *would* be me.

Right, I said. *I'm not going back there. I'd rather starve. I'm going to buy a one-way ticket to London, a bicycle, and a tent. And I'm going to cycle from London to Greece in search of the promised land.*

But what about money, a little voice wanted to know. You don't have any.

It was true. I had a few thousand dollars saved, but no other significant assets. I didn't own my own home and I didn't have a car. While my peers had spent their twenties and thirties building careers, feathering their nests, investing sensibly in property, and generally getting ahead, I'd been a student, a perpetual one, and I'd stayed a student far longer than I should have, because of a sneaking suspicion that the traditional working world wasn't going to suit me at all.

For my reward, I now had the most useless doctorate in the world, having spent ten years examining church doctrine and trying to figure out what was wrong with it. There really wasn't a lot I could do with a doctorate in doctrine, so I became for a while a bookseller. A spectacularly unsuccessful bookseller, I might add. And then I'd ended up in the Ministry of Human Misery, a situation that confirmed all my previous suspicions about how unsuited I was to a conventional working life.

I was single. I'd never married. I had a son who I'd raised single-handed, but he'd recently flown the nest. Perhaps the only advantage in having nothing and no-one was the freedom it gave me to do what I pleased. My sole travelling companion would be God. Okay, he didn't say much, but I trusted that when it really mattered he'd show up with a lightning bolt, a burning bush, or perhaps to part the Aegean Sea.

[Note to atheists and agnostics: There is no gratuitous religion in this book. Religious references are only included where relevant or necessary to the unfolding of the story.]

I lay in that hospital bed for three weeks, dreaming about the life that awaited. I'd become a hermit. I'd find a cave somewhere — in the Greek mountains perhaps. I'd live there all alone because that's what hermits do, and I'd write books. There'd be no electricity, so I'd have to write them longhand, but they would be so amazing, there'd be publishers lining up to publish them.

For food I'd live off the land, a tomato here, an aubergine there. It would be the simple life I'd craved ever since I could remember. It would be wonderful. I'd become a legend. When I was dead people would say "Did you know she lived in that cave in the mountains for twenty years…?" And they'd organize pilgrimages to visit the cave, and when they got there they'd be healed of their diseases…. Oh yes, it was going to be the biggest, fattest, Greek midlife crisis anyone had ever had.

But I had to get out of hospital first.

The specialist threw a fit. He was one of those prim and prissy young men who had never been a child, who had come out of the womb a fully mature adult, and who thought just because he was a medical man he had the right to sit in moral judgement on an insane middle-aged woman. There's one in every hospital.

I thought it might be sensible to carry a letter with me just in case I had a relapse and needed to present something to a foreign doctor, so I told him of my plans and asked him to write me a referral letter.

He wrote the letter with pursed lips and a disapproving look, and then he put it in a sealed envelope and handed it to me as if I was a child and this was my school report, to be opened only by my parents. But I opened it anyway, because I was not a child. When I read it I saw why he'd sealed it. It said rude things prefaced with phrases like: "Against my better judgement….Ignoring my advice…..When the inevitable occurs…."

I handed in my resignation the day I returned to the Ministry, and worked out my notice in a drugged haze, still tanked up on hospital medication. Perhaps it's a bit of an exaggeration to say that I worked out my notice. I did almost no work at all, but they'd lost interest in me by then, and I got away with it.

In the evenings and at weekends I sold my collection of books on the internet and scraped together more money for my trip, aided in this matter by my son Michael, the only person in the family who ever had any of the stuff. Then I made the necessary purchases for my adventure: there was the lightweight sleeping bag, the lightweight tent, the fancy camera, the pannier bags, the self-inflating mattress and the tiny spirit stove that was no larger than a can of baked beans.

I couldn't afford a new laptop, so I was stuck with the oldest and heaviest device in the world. It didn't even have wireless capability, something that was going to cause a great deal of unnecessary difficulty once I was on the road.

And of course there was the most significant purchase of them all. The bicycle. The thing that I had no idea how to ride.

The day I bought the bicycle I had a panic attack — not a figure-of-speech panic attack, but a real panic attack, attended by hyperventilation, nausea, and giddiness.

I knew nothing of bicycles. I hadn't ridden one since I was about seven, and hadn't been very good at them then. Bicycles had changed a lot since those days, too: they now had gears. Mine had twenty-one of them and I had no idea how they worked or what they did. And I was planning to ride this terrifying thing from London to Greece.

I still don't know what gear I was in as I cycled through Europe, which, in retrospect, probably explains quite a lot. It certainly explains the problems I had with hills, but more of that later. For now, the bicycle sat unused in my living room, all sparkly new and black and silver and winking at me spitefully. I'd wake up in the middle of the night, sweating and shaking, after yet another bicycle nightmare involving careering downhill on a silver and black machine that was wildly out of control.

When I wasn't busy with all that I consumed all the published accounts I could lay my hands on of other people who'd also lost their minds and done similar things. There was the man who'd left his home in Germany sometime in the 1960s, intending to cycle round the world just once, but who never went home. He just kept on going round and round the world, surviving on pennies a day, and selling slides of his photographs from time to time to get by.

Then there was retired British headmistress, Anne Mustoe (now deceased), who set off from London on her bicycle at the age of 55 to see the world. Like me she was unfit, although probably not nearly as unfit as I was. Like me she didn't know one end of the bicycle from another, and like me was travelling on a modest budget, although not nearly as modest as mine.

I liked Anne Mustoe and her belief that possessions made us their prisoner, and that human beings really need very little in this life: just shelter, food and water. Anything beyond that is an encumbrance. That being said, if her written accounts were anything to go by, Mrs Mustoe exchanged water for wine at every available opportunity.

I also liked the way she believed that if you strode forth (or cycled forth) into the world confidently, expecting the best from people, that is what you would get. She was the sort of woman, who, if confronted by an armed brigade of Taliban fighters, would have told them to stop being silly and put down their guns. And they would have done so. I was not nearly as indomitable as Mrs Mustoe and I knew it. Anne Mustoe would not have had a panic attack when buying her bicycle.

What have I done? I said to God. *What was I thinking? Why didn't you stop me?*

God said nothing, but a picture flashed into my mind of a vine groaning with grapes, which I found vaguely reassuring, because it was not a picture of a mangled bicycle at the bottom of a cliff. From that vision, rightly or wrongly, I derived the vague impression that God somehow approved of this madness, although I am willing to concede this was merely an hallucinatory side-effect from all the medication.

There were of course a number of quite serious flaws in the plan, aside from the obvious one that I was planning to ride from London to Greece on a bicycle, was terrified of bicycles, and didn't know how gears worked.

The second major flaw in the plan was money. I had worked out an optimistic budget: if I spent just €15 a day, it would be six months before I starved. It was the sort of budget with no room for maneuver, no room for emergencies and one that meant I'd have to earn money as I went along to supplement it.

I was taking a wild gamble, setting in motion a great spin of the roulette wheel in that I was backing myself to make enough money from my writing to keep going. It was effortless in theory: I pictured a stream of published articles flowing in my wake, and fat cheques rolling into my bank account. If we knew in advance how reality was going to differ from our dreams, I don't think any of us would have the courage to get out of bed in the morning.

The third flaw in the plan was Polly, because Polly did not like the idea at all.

Polly was my indomitable 80-year-old mother and she was not at all happy. Her only daughter was planning to travel to the other side of the world in order to ride a bicycle across Europe and sleep in a tent.

"Why don't you just get a *bus* to Athens, darling, if you must go at all, it will be so much more comfortable," she said.

"It wouldn't be the same," I said, and explained how the whole point of the expedition was that it should be uncomfortable, an adventure, a wild pedal thrust into the unknown.

When the appeal to comfort didn't work, she changed tack, and tried emotional blackmail instead. "What will I do without you?" she wailed. "I shall be so worried. I shall be so lonely, here all by myself."

She had a point, too, for I'd be leaving Polly in a retirement village, and God knows it was one of the most depressing places on earth; the sort of place people dump their old folk to live out their last few years and then die.

Polly told me a story about one of her fellow inmates, which just about sums up everything there is to say about places such as those. Every morning this poor old soul would pack all her clothes in a suitcase and tell the staff: "My daughter is coming for me today, she's going to take me away to live with her and the family."

But of course the daughter never came. And in the evening the staff would quietly unpack the suitcase until the morning, when the whole process would be repeated. And the next day, and the next.

Now my plans had met maternal opposition of a most determined sort. There seemed only one way to reconcile Polly to the idea. So the next thing I knew, I found myself saying something like this:

"How about when I get to Greece, I'll find us a flat or a cottage or something and you can leave this concentration camp for the elderly, and I'll look after you in your declining years. Would you feel any better about me going if we agreed to do that?"

The attitudinal transformation was instantaneous. Her face, which had been as sour as an old prune, brightened at once, and she went from being the greatest detractor of the plan to its most enthusiastic supporter.

"That sounds lovely, darling," she said. "I shall *love* living in Greece. They have those wonderful pastries called baklava there, and they have that wonderful metaxa brandy. And we shall be together, and we shall be so happy."

Yes," I said. "We shall be so happy." I had to abandon the idea of the cave in the mountains, of course, because an 80-year-old woman needs a few creature comforts, but perhaps the cave hadn't been such a great idea in the first place.

And so we pored together over maps of Greece, and looked at the pictures in my guidebook, and she reminisced about the twenty-four hours she had spent in Athens once on a stopover, and how she'd thought it the most wonderful place in the world.

Now that she had a Greek adventure of her own to look forward to, one that included baklava and metaxa, along with welcome and unexpected parole from Stalag Elderly, Polly began at once her preparations, which largely involved deciding which books had to come to Greece, and which she could manage to do without. She'd sit there all day making lists, happy as a lark, and because she was happy, I was happy, too, because a positive Polly was much easier to deal with than a negative Polly.

Besides, although I had truly meant it, I never thought for one second, deep down, she would *actually* come and live with me in Greece at the age of 80. It was, after all, a land where she would not be able to speak a word of the language, where the medical care would be an unknown quantity, and where she'd be separated from everything and everyone comfortable and familiar. Of course she wouldn't go through with it. I mean, *what a stupid idea.*

Chapter 4: If It Seems Too Good To Be True...

"Today is the Buddha's birthday. To celebrate this special holiday, the government pays for tuk-tuk drivers to take tourists to see all the famous temples in the city for just 10 baht." My new best friend was all smiles. Ten baht was mere pennies in any currency. It seemed too good to be true.

It was my overnight stopover. My boxed bicycle was safely stored at Bangkok International Airport, and I had 24 hours to kill before the flight to London. It was early morning and I was wandering the streets of Bangkok, taking in the sensory overload of sights, sounds and smells. I hadn't been out of New Zealand for twenty years, and it was all quite overwhelming.

I wasn't used to being approached every five steps by someone trying to sell me something. I wasn't used to such cloying heat and humidity. And most of all I wasn't used to con artists. New Zealand is essentially an *honest* country, a land where what you see is what you get.

I am not telling this story simply to fill up space, although it will help do that, but because it would be nice to save just one or two people from falling into the trap that the con artists of Bangkok went to such considerable lengths to set for me.

They didn't know I was skint as a bucket and hence a poor target, of course, but I don't like to think of them succeeding with others where they failed with me. I don't like to think of other innocents abroad, those who might have deeper pockets and more trusting natures, falling prey to what was a very sophisticated and elaborate scam.

My new friend sidled up and introduced himself quite disarmingly. "I am a high school teacher," he said. Occupations don't come more respectable than that. No need to be suspicious of a high school teacher.

What a lovely country Thailand is, I thought, and what a wonderful custom. A guided tour of Buddhist temples on this, the Buddha's birthday. I could have envisaged no more perfect start to my overseas adventure.

"How fortunate you are to arrive on a day such as this! Welcome to Bangkok," he said.

What he really meant was *how fortunate I am to meet a gullible simpleton who will believe every fork-tongued, duplicitous word I utter.*

"The special promotion," he continued, "is limited to yellow government tuk-tuks."

My mind was now fully at rest. Then, as if on cue, and in the first of a series of coincidences that would only make sense later, what should come careering down the street towards us, but a yellow "government" tuk-tuk.

My companion waved down the "government" tuk-tuk driver, who invited me to climb aboard. My driver was young, well-dressed, and affability itself.

"We shall go first," he said, "to visit the Temple of the Great Golden Buddha." And so we set off, bucketing through the choking Bangkok traffic.

It was unbearably hot. A thick blanket of pollution was trapping 35 degree heat and there was no respite from its sweltering oppressiveness. It was early morning, but already I was dripping with sweat. The Great Golden Buddha was worth the discomfort, though. He cut an impressive figure and was indeed both golden and great.

Once I had done gazing at the Great Golden Buddha, I found the tuk-tuk driver waiting, just as he had promised, and we set off again, whizzing from temple to temple.

The morning was going very well. I was certainly getting to see a lot of buddhas, so many, in fact, that after a while my appreciation for the finer points of buddhas in various positions and colours was beginning to wane. Aside from the standing buddha, there was a reclining buddha and countless seated buddhas. They also came in a range of colours with the emerald buddha the most famous.

It was at the temple of the blue buddha that stage two of the scam unfolded. There was a man sitting on a bench outside the temple, an extremely well-dressed man, dripping in jewelry. He smiled at me.

"The temple is closed and will remain so for ten minutes or so," he said. "The monks are still at prayer. Welcome to Thailand, my name is Dr. Han."

I realized later how artfully he directed the conversation. I don't know quite how he did it, but within minutes we were talking about sapphires.

"I am happy this morning," said Dr Han. "I have just made an excellent business transaction. From a reputable wholesaler I have purchased a set of sapphires. Later today I fly to London where I will make a handsome profit, of at least 100 percent, selling them in Covent Garden."

"It is perfectly legal to buy sapphires and sell them overseas," continued Dr Han, whose doctorate was in con artistry, "so long as you tell Customs Officials the jewels are for personal use and retain your authenticity certificate and receipt." He produced a receipt from his pocket and urged me to read it. It appeared "Dr Han" had indeed just spent several thousand dollars on sapphires.

"Tourists do this all the time," he said. "They come to Thailand, where the sapphires are incomparable, and return to Europe where incomparable sapphires are in great demand. Have you have not heard of this? I am astonished!"

I was now starting to feel a little uncomfortable. Faint warning bells were beginning to chime. Then it all got a whole lot more elaborate.

Enter Pierre the Pimp, fake tourist, right on cue. Pierre certainly looked a tourist, complete with camera and souvenir t-shirt that said *I Love Bangkok*. He spoke with a heavy French accent and asked if the temple would be open soon. He and "Dr Han" pretended not to know each other.

He glanced at the receipt "Dr Han" was waving about. "Ah yes," said Pierre the Pimp, "I too have bought sapphires here in Bangkok and sold them in Paris for an excellent profit—several times what I paid for them in fact. This very morning I bought a set."

His story thus corroborated by a 'stranger,' the Doctor of Lies renewed his sales pitch with increased urgency.

"There's a special promotion today at the sapphire wholesalers," he said, rising to take his leave. "It finishes at 11am and now it is already 10.30am. You must go at once or you will miss out!"

Even to my gullible ears the urgency in his voice sounded a little odd—why on earth should the promotion end at 11am? And why should he care if I bought sapphires or not?

The penny dropped fully when our next stop turned out to be the sapphire wholesaler. The tuk-tuk driver urged me to go inside and look around.

"Take your time," he said, "there's no rush." I had no desire to look at sapphires, but it seemed churlish to refuse. He had transported me round Bangkok for several hours, after all, and I'd seen a lot of buddhas for just pennies. It seemed the least I could do.

It was a mistake. I was immediately assailed by the Evil Prince of all Sapphire Salesmen and a retinue of six identically uniformed maidens. Through overbearing strength of numbers they escorted me to an upstairs room where hundreds of sapphires were laid out in glass cases. It was my turn to deceive. I hummed and haahed and pretended to be interested in the damned things. It seemed impolite to do otherwise. But I needn't have worried about offending the Evil Prince, for he was a thoroughly nasty piece of work. The second he figured out I was a time-waster he was as keen to get rid of me as I was to be gotten rid of.

"Did you buy anything?" The tuk-tuk driver's smile wavered uncertainly. I shook my head and he turned from beaming affability to scowling aggression in a millisecond.

"It is finished," he said, shoving me from his tuk-tuk onto some unknown street corner in Bangkok. I mean literally. He quite literally and physically shoved me out of the tuk-tuk.

One safely in England, mercifully sans sapphires, I searched the net and discoed many melancholy web pages devoted to The Great Thai Sapphire Scam. Dozens of tourists had parted with large chunks of money in hope of a quick and juicy profit. The stories were identical: an initial contact with a tout, a Buddha Birthday special, a complicit tuk-tuk driver, an encounter with a stranger in temple gardens, and the appearance of a fake tourist to confirm the story. All this then followed by a visit to the dealer, the purchase of some grossly overpriced gems, and, in a sickening conclusion, the dread news from an expert in Europe that the sapphires were "incomparable" only in their inferiority.

So the moral of the story here is quite simple and obvious really: if it sounds too good to be true, it almost certainly is.

Chapter 5: The Floating Pink Gin Palace

Henry met me at Heathrow and Henry didn't like me very much. This was because Henry didn't suffer fools gladly, and was of the opinion that I fell into that category. My plan to cycle solo across Europe in search of Utopia had something to do with this judgement, I think.

Henry was married to my old friend Clare and when I'd emailed her about my midlife crisis, and my plans for dealing with it, she'd kindly invited me to spend a few days with them in their house near London, before travelling with them to Holland.

It was an irresistible offer, because it meant I'd not have to start my cycle tour in London, where cyclists got flattened on a regular basis. Holland had several other advantages, or so I'd been led to believe: it was completely flat, and was blessed with an excellent network of cycle lanes.

Henry and Clare were travelling to Holland because they'd recently purchased a very large boat there. It was temporarily moored at a marina near the ancient town of Elburg and they were going to get it going, and a few days later sail it north to Monnikendam, where they had secured permanent mooring.

They'd not seen the boat yet, because they'd bought it over the internet. So, after a few days catching up with Clare and getting used to a country where the sun never shone, we travelled through the night to Holland. It all went smoothly except for one minor hiccup on the British side of the channel tunnel, when Henry was given the full treatment: sniffer-dogs, metal and bomb detectors, and would you please unpack the 4x4, sir.

"Well, that's the first time *that's* ever happened to me," Henry said, staring at me accusingly in the rear-view mirror. Then it was through the tunnel and across three countries in a matter of hours, to arrive at Elburg marina along with the dawn.

There were plenty of boats moored at Elburg marina, and there was one ship. The ship was the vessel Henry and Clare had purchased, and it was the sort of thing film stars might own.

On the inside it was all faded grandeur and plush pink and gold décor, and it looked like Barbara Cartland's boudoir. The wallpaper was pink, the deep pile carpets were pink, the velvet upholstery was pink. On every available surface there was a large gold container filled with elaborate displays of artificial pink flowers. There were three double bedrooms (bedrooms, not cabins), no less than two bathrooms, a saloon and a kitchen.

Everything was pink. It was, in fact, a luxurious floating pink apartment. I had lived in apartments that were smaller. I am living in an apartment that is smaller at the moment.

It was because of the pink interior that Clare had fallen in love with it, and the reason they'd bought it. "Isn't it gorgeous, all this pink?"

Who goes on the internet and buys a million pound boat, without seeing it first, just because it's pink?

"It's too bloody pink," said Henry. "It would be a great boat if it weren't so pink."

She used to be called something Dutch, but they'd renamed her. Now she was called *Blessed*. This made me nervous, because it implied God was thrilled, and that everything was going to go perfectly.

So of course everything went wrong. The first thing that went wrong was the electricity, which spluttered, fizzled and died and took two days to fix. We sat in the dark, eating cold food, with Henry glaring at me across the candles as if it was my fault, and wearing his *what is she still doing here* expression.

"You realize, don't you, that cycling around with a tent and a sleeping bag is just asking for trouble?" he said. "It's like advertising to criminals that you're easy prey." I don't think he realized that saying stuff like that, which he did quite often, was making me less, rather than more inclined to leave, and hence exacerbating his other problem with me: the fact that I was there at all.

The next thing that went wrong was the plumbing. The engine room flooded and two more days were devoted to mopping and pumping and locating leaks. This wasn't good for the engine, so there were problems with that, too.

"It would be a great boat if only it bloody worked," said Henry.

It became advisable to avoid Henry as much as possible, so I made day trips into the surrounding countryside while Henry mopped, pumped and swore and Clare said soothing things and poured large medicinal measures of gin and tonic.

On my day trips through the northern stretches of the Netherlands, a vast reclaimed polder called Flevoland, I passed through a barren, desolate and featureless landscape that had been stolen from the sea. I wondered what it would be like to live there, what sort of impact such an empty landscape would have on the character.

Lawrence Durrell wrote about the relationship between people and landscape. He believed that if you removed the entire population of France and replaced the French with Mongolians, within a century or two the Mongolians would have turned into Frenchmen and would behave just as the old French had done.

So strong, he believed, was the connection between landscape and people, that it is location that created national character. (I find it easier to imagine Mongolians becoming Frenchmen than Frenchmen becoming Mongolians, although I am not entirely sure why this is so.)

I wobbled my way through this strange moonscape of a land, getting used to the bicycle, pondering these matters, and sometimes had the greatest difficulty believing I was even there at all, so removed was it from my life in New Zealand.

Meanwhile, back in Elburg, location and landscape were doing little for Henry's character as he wrestled with the ongoing disasters aboard *Blessed*. The toilet disaster was the worst, because toilet disasters usually are. This particular toilet disaster lasted twenty-four hours and does not bear detailed description.

If I'd been responsible for the toilet disaster (I wasn't, Henry was), I'd have just kept on cycling and not ever gone back. You may be wondering why I didn't just do that anyway, given that I had clearly outstayed my welcome, and the *what is she still doing here* looks were becoming more and more frequent. Why didn't I just say "Hey, thanks, it's been lovely, I'm heading off tomorrow"? If I'd had any pride, I'd have done just that.

But the plain truth of the matter is that with each passing day I was growing more and more terrified of the journey ahead, all alone, on a bike, right across Europe with just God and a tent, and fear is a much more powerful force than pride. So I put off leaving, and made the excuse I just *had* to stay long enough for *Blessed*'s inaugural journey. I couldn't possibly miss that! And this in spite of the fact that it would take me north instead of south, and further away from Greece, rather than closer.

"I wouldn't let any of the women in *my* family embark on such a journey," said Henry, with wonderful disregard for more than a century of gender equality. "If I were you, I would buy a bus ticket to Greece and find somewhere to stay as quickly as possible. You can go for day trips on your bicycle if you must…"

Eventually, a week behind schedule and amidst mounting tension, *Blessed* was declared fit to take to the water. To get to Monnikendam we had to negotiate the Dutch lock system and then cross a fairly large stretch of water called the Markemeer. Meer means lake, and a lake did not sound particularly threatening. I consulted the map. Okay, it was a pretty large Meer, to be sure, but it was a Meer no less. And how difficult can a Meer be?

The Markemeer was terrifying. The maiden journey had been terrifying even before we reached the meer's vast and angry expanse. Henry had decided to try out his new auto pilot thing, which had instantly sent *Blessed* careering towards the reedy bank, scattering ducks, and bringing us dangerously close to running aground.

"Oh shit," I said.

Then there was the lock system that had us bumping into and bouncing off the concrete walls, and garnering angry yells from lockkeepers.

"Oh shit," I said, each time we collided with concrete.

Even though technically a lake, the Markemeer was throwing a temper tantrum befitting a child of the North Sea, of which it is a vast inlet. Soon dark waves were slamming into the saloon windows and *Blessed* was exhibiting a gravitational preference for the almost-horizontal. From the shore we must have looked like a Victorian painting entitled 'Shipwreck at Sea."

I clutched the pink armrests of the pink sofa and contemplated a watery grave. Then Henry mentioned that his only previous boating experience had been on a barge on the Thames.

"Oh shit, oh shit, oh shit."

"For shit's sake, will you *stop* saying oh shit," shouted Henry.

"So when are you leaving, then?" he asked, when we finally made safe mooring in Monnikendam, about five minutes before all daylight disappeared and mooring would have become impossible.

"Er, tomorrow morning," I said.

"Good," he said, looking happier than he'd done in days.

I really should thank him. If he hadn't put it like that I'd probably still be there now, cowering beneath one of *Blessed's* pink sofas in the saloon, slurping Henry and Clare's pink gin, and gibbering nervously at the prospect of what lay ahead.

Chapter 6: Holland is Flat and Other Myths

Myth No. 1: Holland is flat. Holland looks flat, but it isn't. There's no other explanation for the fact that sometimes, during those first few days of my Greek midlife crisis, I was able to ride, and at other times I had to get off and push, even though the road looked exactly the same — dead flat — in both instances.

I am not sure why this was. Perhaps it had to do with the fact that the earth is round, or perhaps it was that I am just uniquely sensitive to the curvature of the earth's surface — a bit like the princess and the pea. For it must be admitted that this phenomenon of the non-flatness of the Netherlands did not seem to bother the 90-year olds who flew past me on their antiquated bicycles, jingling their bells in an impatient get-out-of-the-way, you're-taking-up-the-whole-cycle-lane kind of fashion. And it certainly didn't bother the young people who laughed hysterically at the sight, never seen before in the Netherlands, of a cyclist pushing her bike on the flat.

In my defence, this was the first time I'd had a fully-loaded bicycle. Those exploratory trips round Flevoland had been on an unladen one. Cycling hadn't seemed too bad then. I'd hardly had to push the thing at all. But now, just a few miles into my epic adventure, I'd started reviewing the necessity of all those items that had seemed so indispensable just hours before. Did I *really* need *Teach Yourself Spanish* in two volumes, with accompanying CDs, or *Teach Yourself Portuguese* in one volume? And why did I have the heaviest and most antiquated laptop on the planet, the chunkiest camera, the six blank foolscap notebooks, the large pack of maps? The clothes, toiletries, tent, sleeping bag and self-inflating mattress were probably necessities, but the other things? I was starting to doubt it.

This was especially true as I'd now jettisoned plans for that quick detour whizzing through Spain and Portugal en route to Greece. From the comfort of my living room in New Zealand, peering at maps in a small-scale school atlas, Europe had looked compact and manageable. Now that I was here, and even the relatively short distance from Monnikendam to Amsterdam was turning into a marathon well beyond my capabilities, Europe was turning out to be not small and manageable at all. I would have to forget Spain and Portugal and head straight for Greece.

So that meant I wouldn't need *Teach Yourself Spanish.* But I couldn't throw it away, because that would be a waste. So *Teach Yourself Spanish* went with me all the way to Greece, unopened.

Along with the discovery that Europe was quite big, and that roads in the Netherlands weren't flat, there had been one positive to emerge from those first few hours on the road. My pre-departure terror had subsided a great deal. There weren't criminals lurking behind every bush, as Henry had predicted. There were still difficulties, certainly. For example, in order to get to Greece, I was going to have to go through Amsterdam, and in spite of the excellent Dutch cycle paths, I found this a daunting prospect. Everyone else seemed to know what they were doing on those cycle paths, and did it swiftly and efficiently, which was fine for them. What wasn't fine was a phenomenon called cycle path rage, which I'd just learned about, and which tended to be directed at incompetent and slow cyclists who didn't know what they were doing.

But there was no way round Amsterdam; I would have to take it on. Well there was, but a detour round Amsterdam would have added too many kilometers to the journey, and now that I was finally on my way, I was keen to get to Greece as quickly as possible.

So, plucking up all my courage, I joined the thick traffic on the outskirts of the city and got swept along with it, into the urban heart of the place. It took hours to get to the other side. The city seemed to go on forever. And while those canals may have looked straight on the map, they were nothing of the sort, and none of them headed in the direction of Greece. They kept taking me off in a westerly or easterly direction. I could tell because of the way the sun kept slipping round from the right-hand side of the bike where it was supposed to be, and moving somewhere else, either ahead or behind. And this led me to my next scientific discovery about cycling through Europe.

Myth No. 2: Maps are Truthful: It was thus in Amsterdam I had my first inkling that maps are paper-borne lies created to frustrate and confound, having at best only a tenuous relation to reality. On that first day I was led up the garden path by my map at least a dozen times, and sometimes quite literally.

And so it was, not far out of Amsterdam, somewhere just south of Utrecht to be precise, although perhaps it wasn't Utrecht after all, but somewhere else entirely, I reached the second momentous decision of my adventure (after the one about not nipping off to Spain and Portugal), and that was to throw away all my maps.

I had already been lost at least half a dozen times, and had wasted hours on detours that seemed to be taking me back towards Amsterdam. The sun moved a full 180 degrees at one point, and it was the sun that was telling the truth, not the map.

The map had also led me astray in the matter of finding my first campsite for that first night on the road. Darkness fell and I was forced to rent a caravan for the night.

In the comfort of the caravan, feeling guilt-ridden about blowing the best part of a week's budget on four walls and a roof, I made the decision to navigate by the sun. On days when the sun wasn't shining, I would seek direction from the good people I met along the way, and trust my instincts, rather than maps.

Greece was south, more or less, so as long as I kept going in a southerly direction, making sure the sun was on the left of the bicycle in the mornings and on the right in the afternoons, sooner or later I'd get to Greece.

There were additional benefits to this plan. My load would be lighter. The maps weighed a ton, and I was desperate to shed any unnecessary weight. Then there'd be the thrill of not knowing where I was. I'd be forced to get to know lots more locals. I'd have to ask them the whereabouts of the nearest campsite.

On cloudy days I'd have to ask them which way was south. Travelling mapless was going to be fun. But travelling mapless was also going to be directly responsible for the uncovering of a third myth.

Myth No. 3 – Everyone in Europe Speaks English. Not only is this untrue, but can even be stated antithetically. *No-one* in Europe speaks English. I blame Clare and Henry for perpetuating the myth and for lulling me into a false sense of security. On one of our *Blessed* evenings, I'd expressed concern about my linguistic abilities, or lack of them, saying I was worried this was going to be a problem.

"Nonsense," said Clare, with the confidence for which she is famous. "There's absolutely nothing to worry about. *Everyone* in Europe speaks English, and even if they don't, just say something foreign, like *Bonjour*, and you will be fine. I've never had a moment's trouble in Europe and I've never met a soul who doesn't speak English."

If you are travelling about in a car or a ship, and staying in hotels or on ships, bumping into other people who do those kinds of things, then yes, perhaps everyone does speak English in Europe. But if you are travelling in the outer boondocks, cycling through remote villages no-one has ever heard of, in order to avoid motorways, and because you left your maps in Utrecht, well no, it's just not true. They don't speak a word of English in Europe.

Rural Holland was in fact a relatively gentle introduction to the linguistic purgatory to come. Here at least I had my secret weapon, one that would be of no use anywhere else, and one that has never been any use either before or since.

For I grew up in a country where human rights were trampled, and where most of the population lived in misery while an elite few waxed rich: not Britain or America, but South Africa. Somehow I still spoke tolerable Afrikaans, in spite of not having spoken a word of it, not once, not since the age of eighteen, which was the last time I'd been forced to do so.

I have Mrs Van der Saade to thank for this unexpected and forgotten ability. I can still see her grinning in fiendish delight as she humiliated me by sending me to the dunce's seat up at the front of the class. Still for all her faults, or perhaps because of them, she did manage to hammer the basics of Afrikaans into the head of one who conscientiously objected on aesthetic grounds.

But now, in the Netherlands, I was discovering that a language hammered into a young head over an extended period of time is never lost, no matter how unwilling or uninterested the young head. Words, phrases and expressions I had no idea I remembered, let alone knew, tumbled effortlessly from my lips.

And what's more, the good folk of the Netherlands understood me. The only problem was I didn't understand their replies; they were all Dutch to me. This, I suspected, was because Afrikaans developed as an adulterated version of Dutch. When it was exported to South Africa in the seventeenth century, it got stuck in a colonial time warp, and it was a lower form of Dutch to begin with, something called kitchen Dutch, rather than the high Dutch of polite society. And so, due to a lack of synergy, the gap between the two languages widened.

Still, a one-way conversation was better than no conversation at all, and I could at least make my needs and thoughts known. Failure to comprehend the replies made life difficult, but not impossible.

It was my second day on the road. So far Henry's direst predictions had not come to pass; I'd bust a few myths; my body was accustoming itself to the shock therapy; and I was starting to feel quite pleased with myself. I'd now left the heavily industrialized areas around Amsterdam and Utrecht behind, and the landscape began to manifest an ever-changing sweetness, with woodland glades and small lakes and immaculately maintained farmlands. Everywhere there was water in one form or another — this was the Netherlands, after all.

It was time to make the acquaintance of my tent. My tent and I would grow mighty familiar by the time I was done, and I'd come to hate it with a passion, but for now it was new and exciting. It was also scary – at least at first. After all, a tent doesn't offer a great deal of protection against the perils and dangers of the night. Anyone with a will to enter a tent can do so. All they need is a sharp knife and an unpleasant disposition.

It was in my tent, after dark, in those early days, that I'd have some quite intense exchanges with God. "I am scared," I said that first tented night on a farm that had a field turned over for the use of campers. It was early April and this early in the season I was the only camper. Mine was the solitary, badly erected tent in the corner of the vast field. "Please keep me safe till morning."

And God said nothing, because that's what He's like, and so I lay awake for hours hyperventilating. But I went to sleep eventually, because not even terror can keep a person awake all night if they've just cycled more kilometers than can reasonably be expected with such abysmal levels of fitness.

In the morning everything looked so peaceful and safe, and I wondered why I had worried. This was rural Holland, after all. I was camped near a fence, and a whole host of farm animals had gathered on the other side to bid me good morning—a curious and charming band of cows, sheep and horses.

The criminal element of Holland had clearly had better (or worse) things to do in the middle of the night than attack a tiny tent in an obscure farmer's field in the back of beyond. And so it dawned on me gradually in those early days that I was probably, on the whole, safer in my little tent in the countryside than I would have been behind a locked door in one of the cities. If there were other campers, they tended to be elderly folk in campervans and elderly folk in campervans tend not to be dangerous. There probably aren't too many 75-year-old serial killers roaming the campsites of the Netherlands.

Terror at the adventure I had embarked upon (it hadn't seemed nearly so scary in the planning stages), was gradually subsiding, to be replaced with a growing sense of freedom and joy. I loved also the intimate way I was getting back to nature. And there's nothing quite like living in a tent for getting real intimate with nature.

You share it, just for starters, with whatever insect population inhabits that particular region or country. This hadn't occurred to me before I left. I hadn't thought, gosh, I wonder if the insects of the Netherlands are different from the insects of Greece? But oh yes, indeed they are.

And just as my introduction to linguistic purgatory was gentle in the Netherlands, so too was my introduction to nature. From its flat(tish) roads, to its well behaved dogs which were always, always decently restrained behind fences where dogs belong, to its civilized insects, and its charmingly polite farm animals, everything was gentle and well-behaved in the Netherlands.

There was even a goat that said thank you, in one of those believe-it-if-you-like, I'm-not-too-bothered-either-way stories. I was camped for a couple of nights on a farm near a village called Vlymen. Between my tent and the ablutions block was a goat pen, with about ten goats in it, some tethered, some not. I didn't pay much attention to them, nor they to me. But on my second evening, as I passed by I heard a series of strangled cries and screams. One of the goats had managed to wind its tether-rope about its neck several times.

It was bucking and writhing in panic, and every movement was causing the rope to constrict more tightly. It was already half strangled. Our eyes met and I read there a desperate appeal for help. Too afraid to enter the pen (do goats bite?) I ran instead to fetch the farmer, who was in the middle of his dinner, and not at all thrilled at the interruption. He stomped off towards the goat pen tutting with annoyance, and I thought nothing more of it.

But the next morning, when I walked past the pen, the same goat, now untethered, left his companions and came running to the fence to greet me. He was uttering sounds such as I had never heard before or since, from a goat or from any creature and again our eyes met.

It was an extraordinary moment, because I knew that somehow he had made the connection between his strangled appeal and the farmer's arrival to free him and now he was saying thank you.

Those early days of my trip, cycling through an unusually warm spring, along tree-lined country roads, with no company whatsoever besides curious farm animals, were days of pure joy. I was starting to have the time of my life, which brings me to the fourth myth.

Myth No. 4 – Holland is Boring. I'd fully expected to find Holland boring as blazes. But there was nothing boring about Holland. Even the names weren't boring. How could anyone be bored in a country that had a village called *Beek en Donk?*

As I travelled south, the countryside had started to look oddly familiar. I could have sworn I'd seen that tree-lined road, that field, that windmill, somewhere before. Being mapless, it took longer to dawn on me than it should have, that without the slightest forethought or planning I'd entered the province of North Brabant.

And yes, I had seen that windmill, that row of trees, and possibly even the grandfather of that peasanty-looking chap digging over there, and I had seen them in the paintings of Vincent Van Gogh, for I was now cycling through Van Gogh country.

I had always been enamoured with Vincent Van Gogh, which isn't nearly as crazy as it might sound. Lots of women are in love with dead people. Take Elvis, for example, thousands of women are in love with him, and he's also dead.

Ever since reading *Dear Theo*, the abbreviated edition of Van Gogh's letters, at the age of fifteen, I'd wanted to visit the Van Gogh Museum in Amsterdam and see the great man's art in the paint, so to speak. On Toilet Crisis day I did so, and discovered there was no comparison between reproductions of Van Gogh's paintings (with which I was familiar) and the originals. Nothing could have prepared me for their cyclonic emotional impact — and if I'd realized I was going to weep my way round the museum, to the consternation of those around me, I'd have had the good sense to go armed with tissues.

"I just don't *get* Van Gogh," Henry said, giving me an *are you back already* look when I returned to *Blessed* after my day in the Museum. This led me to suspect Van Gogh was a bit like marmite: you either got him or you didn't.

And now here I was, gliding in a dream through a living Van Gogh landscape, surrounded by the same natural forms, shapes and colours that had inspired his early works. I was happy as a skylark, waving enthusiastically at startled locals, just because they bore some faint resemblance to the people he'd painted.

That being said, poor Van Gogh didn't have nearly as happy a time of it in Van Gogh country as I did. He'd returned to Nuenen because things hadn't worked out in Drenthe, where he'd been before that, or in The Hague, where he'd been before Drenthe, and because he tended to spend his life going from place to place, and leaving in a hurry when things didn't work out.

In Nuenen the not-working-out was all pretty painful. He fell out with his family in a devastatingly permanent way. The rift between Van Gogh and his mother and most of his siblings except Theo and Wilhelmina, would never be healed.

At the root of the problem were rows with his pastor father over the nature of Christianity, his refusal to attend church, and his inability to hold down a proper job. Relations with the local community were strained also, especially when the local Catholic priest forbade members of his congregation to pose for the artist as models. He was accused of fathering a peasant woman's child, (something he strenuously denied), and he was ultimately blamed for hastening his father's unexpected death from a heart attack.

It felt a privilege to be cycling through the same villages and along the same country roads he'd known so well. It felt oddly moving to sit in the same places he had sat to draw and to paint. The little church in Nuenen where his father had ministered, and that he had painted several times, looked just the same in real life as it did in his paintings. I sat on the grass, just about where he would have sat, and listened to 'Jesus Christ is Risen Today' pealing out from the tiny bell tower.

I lingered some days in Nuenen where, along with falling out with just about everybody it was possible to fall out with, Van Gogh had painted his most famous work of the period: *The Potato Eaters*.

Everywhere there were reminders of just why Nuenen existed in the way that it did. There were Van Gogh monuments, Van Gogh guided walks and the somewhat disappointing Van Gogh Documentary Centre. I walked along Van Gogh streets, and stood and stared at a giant sized reproduction of *The Potato Eaters* emblazoned on the façade of one of the public buildings. The town that had once rejected him was now drawing its sustenance from his legacy.

I found it quite ironic really, that they'd rejected him, and now made their living from him, with the layers of irony going quite deep. *The Potato Eaters*, a work that caused an artist acquaintance to complain that Van Gogh had deliberately chosen the ugliest possible subjects, was intended to show the cost of toil. He wanted to demonstrate how the people were connected to the earth, how they ate its produce with the very hands that had brought it into being and how, because of their toil, they were utterly deserving of their evening meal.

So it was interesting to see that while potatoes were still a staple of the region, and that while there were whole aisles given over to the potato in contemporary Dutch supermarkets, they had been completely transformed into these real fancy unpotatoey things. There had been a revolution in the eating of potatoes. It was almost as if the Dutch wanted to disguise the fact that deep down they were still Potato Eaters.

I had not known there were so many different ways of concealing the potato-ness of potatoes. They came ready-peeled, and pre-cut into literally dozens of different shapes and sizes, all designed to make them look like anything but. There were potatoes in triangles, circles, squares, stars, moons, and they were all parboiled and vacuum packed and not an earthy potato peel in sight.

The way they were farmed had also been revolutionized, of course, with no more need for Vincent's iconic sower, or that ox drawn plough. And with the greater prosperity that accompanies mechanization, there had come well-maintained farm houses to replace the humble shacks of Vincent's peasant paintings.

What had remained the same was the colour of the landscape, the soft light, and something about the people themselves. While on the surface it seemed that Van Gogh's peasants were lost forever in their contemporary kitchens, with their running water and electricity, and their potatoes shaped like daisies, every now and then I'd catch a glimpse of inter-generational continuity. I'd see an old woman bent over a flower bed, or a young man digging a ditch, and I'd swear I was looking at the great grandchild of one of Vincent's models, and perhaps I was.

Other continuities existed, if in a somewhat attenuated way. Life continued to revolve around the church, the shop and café, and Sunday was still an obligatory day of rest. The sheer numbers coming and going from church on Sundays astonished me. Wasn't this Holland? Wasn't this the land where you could die on demand, smoke pot at will, and generally do precisely what you pleased? The Netherlands were more complex than I'd ever imagined.

And they were more religious than I'd anticipated, too. Near a village called Mariahout, I chanced upon the tiniest chapel I have ever seen, only fractionally larger than my bicycle, with room for just two chairs, an altar and a tiny lectern. I stopped there to rest and saw on the tiny lectern a book and a pen where visitors recorded their requests to the Almighty. My kitchen Dutch permitted me to read and understand these simple pleas and it was like reading letters to Santa Claus, only more touching, because these where the letters of adults, not children.

Dear God, Please give my wife the strength to overcome her sickness.

Dear God, Please help our family through these difficult times.

Most poignant was the message that simply said *Help!*

I took weeks to cross Holland in the direction of Belgium, a ridiculously long time, considering the short distances involved. I could have done it in a matter of days, but I loved it so much, I didn't want to rush. I was starting to feel a lot better, physically too. After two weeks I had thrown away those six different kinds of medication the specialist told me I would need for life. It felt good to prove him wrong, prissy prat that he was, because it's always satisfying to prove Doubting Thomases and nay-sayers wrong.

I was so very sorry to leave the Netherlands. Some intuition told me it would be a while before life would again be so unvaryingly good. And this turned out to be the case, because the next country between me and Greece was Belgium, and as most people know, nothing good has ever come out of Belgium.

Chapter 7: In Belgium They Stalk Cyclists

I didn't like Belgium, and this is not, I believe, an uncommon reaction to that country. Henry liked Belgium a lot, and that was probably as good a reason as any to dislike the place. But I was soon to be given a much more compelling reason for my dislike than mere contrariness.

In Belgium they stalk cyclists. They drive nasty black cars with tinted windows and stalk cyclists. Not all Belgians, of course, but that's the way of negative experiences: we, or at least I, tend to generalize from them. At any rate, rightly or wrongly, that's how I will always think of Belgium: as that place where not even unfit middle-aged cyclists fast approaching their sell-by date are safe from the activities of stalkers.

And it wasn't a quick stalk, either. My stalker followed me for at least twenty kilometers, and he had to stalk very slowly to accomplish this feat, because he was in a car and I was on a bicycle. But he was nothing if not committed to the task.

Earlier that morning, I'd followed the sun south from a peculiar southern Dutch city called Weert and crossed the border into Belgium. Weert was peculiar not because of any inherent peculiarity, or even because of its weird name, but simply because I could see no good reason why anyone would choose to live there.

It seemed to be a town without a *raison d'être*. Presumably it had one, but what that might have been was not evident to a random passing cyclist.

Cycling along a quiet country road, I crossed the border into Belgium almost without realizing it. There were no signs, no customs posts, no police checkpoints, no passport control. The only way I knew for sure I'd left Holland and was now in Belgium was because of the way the neatly maintained tarmac of the Dutch side deteriorated dramatically into a potholed and shabby concrete mess on the Belgian side. It was as if the efficient Dutch road menders had painted a line across the road and said *we go this far and no further. From this line on, demarcated with our usual Dutch precision, it's Belgium's problem.* And Belgium clearly wasn't too bothered about the problem.

There were other equally noticeable differences that manifest themselves shortly after I'd exchanged impeccable Dutch roads for not so impeccable Belgian ones. The farmhouses were no longer neatly fenced and immaculate. They were run down and dilapidated. The land was empty and desolate, and the woodlands had developed a wild Hansel and Gretel look.

In the Netherlands, every single tree was pruned with military precision, and not a branch permitted to grow beneath head height. In Belgium, nature — trees and weeds in particular — seemed to enjoy a much greater freedom. Yet paradoxically, and Belgium seemed full of paradoxes, nature was just about the only thing to enjoy freedom, because it also became quickly apparent that this was a land of prohibitions.

A day into Belgium and I had seen more signs prohibiting this and that than in my entire time cycling through the Netherlands. *You shall not Enter. It is Forbidden to approach the Worksite. Smoking is forbidden. Using the Station Lift is forbidden,* and, most striking of all, in the bathroom of the campsite in Opglabbeek a sign in bold letters, which, along with prohibiting a whole range of other activities, proclaimed that: *It is forbidden to wash your dog in the sink.*

This sign caused me to wonder if they had had a problem with excessive dog-washing in the sink, or whether it was just that someone had sat down to think through all the various prohibited activities people might be tempted to carry out in the sink and come up with this one.

Opglabbeek was every bit as awful as its name suggests, and the campsite was one of the creepiest places I stayed; so bad, in fact that I left before dawn with a shuddering backward glance. All in all it was a desolate place, this province of Belgium called South Limburgh, and I had an equally desolate time of it, cycling fruitlessly round ghostly villages in search of a bakery, a supermarket – anywhere at all that might sell food. I was hungry. I had not eaten since Weert. But the shops were all boarded up, and with evidence of failed enterprises everywhere, Limburgh appeared to be sunk in a severe economic depression.

My diary entry for that first day in Belgium was just one sentence: "Plan for tomorrow: head as far south as possible as quickly as possible..." My nightly communion with the Almighty included the words 'Please get me out of here.' I had forgotten what happened the last time I'd made that particular request.

As it turned out, I was going to head a lot further south a lot more quickly than expected the following day. But before I did so, Belgium set out to deliver a few quick shocks, as if determined to get rid of me, as if deciding I did not belong there, a judgement with which I heartily concurred.

One of the ongoing necessities of the trip, alongside the food that Belgium was determined to deny me, was regular internet access. I could do without food if I had to, and in Belgium I had to, but a daily visit to some or other facility where I could send and receive emails, was an absolute necessity.

If I were ever to do the trip again, which I won't, because I'm not that stupid, I would make sure I had a laptop that was wireless capable, rather than the oldest and heaviest laptop in the world. I might just as well have carried a manual Olympia typewriter around Europe, for all the use it was. A manual Olympia typewriter may well have been lighter, in fact.

As in so many other respects, in the matter of internet access, the Netherlands had been exemplary. Every public library had computers with internet, and some of the campsites I stayed in did also. It wasn't free, but at least it existed.

In northern Belgium they weren't too bothered about libraries. It took a large chunk of the second day to find one. Eventually, in some godforsaken Belgian town, I stumbled on a library, complete with an inviting row of unoccupied computers. The last time I'd checked my emails was in Holland and I was desperate to make contact with parts of the world that were not Belgium.

"I am sorry," said the librarian. "You must be a member of the library to use the internet."

"But I am travelling," I said. "And I desperately need to check my emails. Would it be possible to use it as a guest?"

"I am sorry," she said again. "That is the rule. It is forbidden to use the internet unless you are a member."

"Perhaps I could become a temporary member?"

"Yes, certainly you may become a temporary member," she said. "But first I will need proof of your residence in Godforsakenbelgiantown."

"But I am not a resident," I said, "I am just travelling. Is there any way around it? Can you possibly make an exception, just for half an hour, just this once, so I can check my emails? It's important…please…."

"I am sorry. If I make an exception for you, I must make an exception for everyone. Unless you are a member, it is forbidden to use the internet…."

Of course there was no internet café either, for we are talking about Godforsakenbelgiantown here, so I had to walk away from the row of unused machines in the unused library, while the librarian smirked self-righteously because she had not been even remotely tempted to break the rules in the interests of human kindness. But this was Belgium, after all, where it was forbidden to wash your dog in the sink, so fat chance of a stranger being allowed to check her emails on one of the dozen unused machines in the unused library.

It's probably starting to sound as if I have a 'thing' about Belgium, that I am some sort of rabid anti-belgian. So I shall hasten to balance that impression by pointing out that there was at least one good thing about Belgium, and that was its cycle network, an excellent system of paths and tracks that allowed me to avoid traffic-laden highways and byways. These were pleasant paths mostly, winding through farmland, but occasionally less pleasantly, through woodland, and Belgian woods, as previously noted, at least in South Limburgh, were decidedly creepy.

Every few kilometers in this complex network there was a junction, where the cycle path intersected with a minor traffic-bearing road. At the junction I would usually find three or four numbered paths going off in different directions. It was a simple system—I consulted one of the charts helpfully posted at each junction, made a note of the numbers I needed to follow in order to reach my destination, and then it was just a matter of biking-by-numbers. I didn't even need a map. In fact a map would have been a positive disadvantage, because it would probably have sent me off in the wrong direction. (Refer myth no. 2 in the previous chapter.)

I had set off early from Opglabbeek in the direction of the unattractively named Genk, taking in along the way Godforsakenbelgiantown, where I'd made the abortive attempt to use the internet. The only reason I was going to Genk was because it lay between Opglabbeek and Greece

. At first the journey was enjoyable, the land was fairly flat; at worst it undulated slightly, and the countryside was attractive in its Belgian way.

I couldn't help noticing that the cycle paths were passing through deserted woodlands where the trees closed in overhead, transforming them into dark and oddly threatening places. I began to feel nervous for the first time in nearly three weeks of cycling. Perhaps I was already unconsciously aware of the presence of my stalker, who could have followed me all the way from Opglabbeek, for all I knew. Or maybe I picked him up in Godforsakenbelgian town.

Wherever I acquired him, the first time I consciously registered his presence, he was parked by the side of the road at one of the cycle junctions. I only noticed the parked car because it was an empty stretch of road and there was no obvious reason for anyone to park there. At that point I had just a vague unformed awareness of an occupied car parked in the middle of nowhere for no apparent reason. People sometimes stop to use their mobile phones — perhaps the driver was taking a call, or consulting a map, or having a cup of coffee. So I turned down my designated path, and gave no more thought to the little black car.

A few kilometers further on I reached another junction, and there, parked at the intersection, was a little black car. My awareness now shifted up a gear, but I still wasn't panicking. Perhaps it wasn't even the same car. Perhaps it was just coincidence. I peered through the tinted glass as I passed, trying to catch a glimpse of the occupant, and had a fleeting impression of someone bald and swarthy, although the swarthiness may well have been an effect of the tinted glass.

I entered the next section of my route which was a narrow lane between fields and as I did so Baldy also pulled off. This particular section of the cycle path was not wide enough to take a car, which was reassuring, but I was becoming increasingly alarmed, as I was still a fair way from Genk and there were more wooded bits to get through.

At the next junction, and the one after that, mild alarm escalated into hyperventilating panic, because both times Baldy and his black car were parked a few meters from the crossroads. This was a section of the cycle path that was especially creepy. It was deserted and dark with forest trees joining overhead, and to make matters worse, it was wide enough to take a car. I pedaled down it like a madwoman, glancing over my shoulder as I went.

Eventually the network terminated in the unprepossessing outskirts of Genk, and there, waiting for me, was my one man reception committee. It was thus a profound relief to see Genk ahead of me, and while I doubt anyone else has ever rejoiced at the sight of Genk, there's a first time for everything. At least in a town I would be safe, although there were still some worrying issues. What if he followed me to my next campsite, which might turn out to be another spooky, under occupied place, just like Opglabbeek?

Please protect me so Henry can't say I told you so when my bloodied corpse is found in some seriously scary Belgian campsite, I said to God, who said nothing, so I kept pedaling on through the streets of Genk, because to get to Greece, I had to go right through Genk and pick up a cycle path on the other side. I glanced behind a few times, but in amongst all the busy Genkians dashing about in their cars, there was no further sign of the little black car. He's given up, I thought, oh good.

Then, unexpectedly the strap that attached my two panniers to the rear bike rack snapped, and panniers and bedroll and tent and everything else spilled out across the road, causing temporary mayhem among the motorists of Genk. There was nothing for it but to stop, gather everything up, and do some makeshift repairs.

As I swung round to see what had happened to my scattered luggage, I caught a brief glimpse of a black car nosing its way into a parking space some hundred meters behind. No-one got out. Had the strap not broken I may not have noticed him in the midst of all the bustle of Genk. I may have shrugged it off and attempted the next section of deserted cycle paths. I may, in fact, have given Henry the opportunity to say I told you so at my funeral.

Looking back, I see that as one of many moments of grace I experienced. God might not have said much, but when push came to shove, He was there, keeping me safe, or, as the twenty-third psalm puts it, being my shepherd, keeping me from want, and guiding me as I cycled through the valley of the shadow of death, otherwise known as Belgium.

And here He was in Genk, alerting me to what, in retrospect, was quite possibly a serious danger. My heart was pounding. There's something so very disturbing about being stalked. The only other time I'd been stalked was just as disturbing, although in a different way. I was a university student at the time, and my stalker lived in the flat above. He'd developed an obsessive crush on me, but it wasn't a regular crush, it was a profoundly creepy one. He followed me around campus and stared at me from slightly mad blue eyes. It all came to a climax when, one memorable day, he painted a large red question mark on my door.

I am not sure what the question was, but I am fairly certain that whatever it was, the answer was No. And rather than hang around and find out, I went and lived somewhere else.

But now I was busying myself with straps and bags and scattered bedroll, deliberately not looking directly in the direction of the little black car, managing nevertheless, to keep a surreptitious, squinted eye on it. It took fifteen minutes to fix the gear and I was not in a hurry. I wanted to give him a chance to move on. But he didn't, and still no-one got out.

At last I was ready to get moving again and wheeled the bike slowly onwards, still keeping a squinted eye behind me. Immediately the little black car was also on the move, crawling along behind me, not overtaking like everyone else. He overtook me at the next cycle path junction — a junction that would put me on a path out of town, and back into what now seemed terrifyingly deserted countryside.

It was not a difficult decision. I had disliked Belgium even before Baldy. So I made an abrupt u-turn, stopped a passerby and asked the way to the station.

I do not know what my stalker had in mind. It would have been obvious from my luggage — bedroll and so on — that I was carrying a tent, and hence camping. It is possible he was following to see where I planned to camp for the night. I'd have been easy prey in a campsite at that time of year, for that early in the spring I was often as not the only camper in the place. But whatever his intentions, I figured it was unlikely they were honourable, and I had no intention of finding out just how dishonourable they might be.

At Genk station I purchased a ticket to a place called Arlon from a surly ticket seller, which is a bit of a tautology, although this particular ticket seller was even more surly than usual.

The railway options from Genk were sorely limited, and the only trains into France itself would take me to parts of France I had no desire to go. So I contented myself with a ticket to the southernmost possible point of Belgium that was bordering on France — the city of Arlon. It was by no means a direct route, for it involved a lengthy detour and a change of train at Brussels.

The train for Brussels was due to depart from the platform furthest away from the station concourse. Accessing this distant platform involved maneuvering my laden bicycle down a very long and steep flight of stairs into the subterranean subway passage system, and then up another interminable flight of stairs on the other side onto the far platform.

For a muscly man this might not have been a problem. But I was not a muscly man and for me it posed a significant problem. The only way to do it was to unload the bicycle, lug my gear down the stairs in two trips, then return for the bicycle, reload it again, wheel it through to the foot of the upward stairway, and then repeat the process.

I assessed the unpleasantness of the task on this, my first (but sadly not last) train ride with bicycle in Europe, before spotting with joy a conveniently placed goods elevator that would do the trick nicely. I wouldn't have to unload a thing, and I wouldn't have to lug a thing.

"May I please use the goods elevator," I asked the surly ticket seller. "My bicycle is very heavy and it will be very difficult to get it up and down those stairs."

His face transformed with sadistic pleasure. "It is forbidden for passengers to use the goods elevator," he said. It made him so happy to say that. It wasn't often life afforded an extra opportunity to make life difficult for someone else, and presumably a Friday afternoon in a ticket booth on Genk Station doesn't get much better than that. Or perhaps he was the brother of the stalker. Either way, if ever out of a job, he should apply to the Ministry of Human Misery, where he'd feel right at home.

It was unfortunate really, this stalker-driven-train business, because it gave me a taste for cheating. Before I left New Zealand, I'd been determined not to cheat, not once. I was going to cycle all the way to Greece, no matter how unpleasantly tall the mountains or how inclement the weather. But the thing with cheating is, once you've done it once, it becomes almost irresistibly tempting to do it again, and from Genk in Belgium all the way to Rimini in Italy, it was a temptation I succumbed to more than once.

Once in Greece I stopped cheating, but this was only because there were no trains, and bicycles weren't allowed on buses. But all that was in the future. For now I was incarcerated for the duration of my first cheating expedition in the bicycle carriage of a train bound for Brussels. The bicycle carriage was a windowless affair with seats facing inward, and the only view was of my bicycle, and other people's bicycles, so I have no idea what Belgium looks like between Genk and Brussels.

Then followed a three hour wait at Brussels North Station, which included another bicycle-lugging trek through the underground passageway to the furthest, distant platform. Here my struggles were observed, impassively, by numerous able-bodied, Belgian gentlemen.

On the train from Brussels to Arlon I found myself sitting beside a large, jovial man from Iceland, and immediately we found we had something in common. He didn't like Belgium either.

"I do not like Belgium," he said loudly in the middle of a carriage packed to the gunnels with Belgians. "It is a terrible place." From the darkening expressions of those around us, I gathered that quite a lot of people understood English in Belgium, even if they refused to speak it. The man from Iceland was impervious to the mounting hostility around us.

"It's a dump," he continued. "The worst of the Benelux trio."

He was a lovely man with impeccable taste in countries, and when the train pulled into Arlon, he even helped me offload my bicycle. Take note, men of Belgium, that's how it's done.

Arlon was the modest capital of the French-speaking Belgian province of Luxembourg. It was twinned with Market Drayton in the United Kingdom and Sulphur in the United States, which is probably all that needs to be said about it. It did, however, boast a splendid Gothic church that dominated the skyline for miles around, and I believe there were the remains of the oldest Roman defensive wall in Belgium around there somewhere, but I wasn't sufficiently excited by the sound of these to explore further.

This fragment of fortification does point to the perils of building a town in the middle of permanently disputed territory, however. Whenever a European war kicked off, Arlon was often one of the first places to be invaded. The area was incorporated in turn into Luxemburg, France and the Netherlands, before becoming part of the sovereign state that is Belgium in 1831.

Darkness had long since fallen in Arlon and there was no campsite that I knew of, but that was okay, because I was right off Belgian campsites. So I wandered the gloomy streets looking for inexpensive lodgings. I found a seedy-looking hotel sufficiently run-down to be inexpensive (although these two things did not necessarily go together). It was indeed cheap and it was indeed seedy, with worn crimson carpets, shabby furnishings, dark wood-paneled walls and steep flights of narrow stairs. The water was lukewarm and the hand basin cracked, but it was clean and Le Patron was kindness itself, singlehandedly redeeming his nation from its cyclist stalkers, unhelpful librarians and surly ticket sellers

I joined Le Patron and a couple of his regulars in the shabby little hotel bar where we drank some wine and they humoured my pitiful attempts at speaking French. (Arlon was in the French-speaking region of Belgium.)

Le Patron then pressed upon me an antiquated map, complete with a penciled route, to help me find my way across the border and into France. The map turned out to be quite useless, but no more so than any other map before or since, and I did not tell my host I had no faith in it.

"Ou est la France, s'il vous plait?" I found myself asking for the umpteenth time next morning, because France was proving strangely elusive. I should have found it hours ago and I was desperate to do so. This was an unexpected setback because France was very large and, according to all accounts, also very close.

France was not much more than ten kilometers from Arlon, in fact, and if I'd taken the main road, I'd have been there in no time. But I didn't do main roads, because they were frightening. Quiet country roads tended also to have their disadvantages, however: they would wander off in directions I'd not been planning on taking. They'd start off going south, but then they'd change their minds, and go west or east, or even north. It was because of country roads that I now found myself not in France, but in a little Belgian village called Halanzy.

The countryside around Halanzy was all pleasant hills, woodland and every now and then a church spire rising heavenward announced the presence of a village. I was getting to know it all quite well, after going round and round in circles in search of France.

Halanzy itself consisted of a village square, a few houses and a pub. There were outdoor tables where I refreshed myself with a cold drink. "Down that road, over that hill and you will find France…" said the waiter, making it sound so simple.

The road he sent me down was dark with overhanging ancient forest, narrow and deserted. Surely this could not be the road to France?

"Non, non," said a woman out walking her dog. "This road just goes into the woods." She didn't know where France was either, but offered to try and help me find it. Back to the intersection we went, the lady and her dog, the bicycle and I.

She stepped into the middle of the road, held up her hand in an imperious gesture, and proceeded to stop all passing traffic. Soon we had a rural traffic jam of French-speaking Belgians, all arguing fiercely, and all offering contradictory directions to France.

The road to France eventually turned out to be the next but one turning to the left and so I climbed the hill, or rather, pushed my bicycle over the hill, and then freewheeled down the other side and into France.

The first indication I was in France was a traffic sign informing motorists they were now free to travel as recklessly as they liked. This was not the exact wording, but it was the effect, which just goes to show the grass is not necessarily greener over the hill in France, when eventually you find it.

I wept when I cycled over the border. I thought this was because I had entered some sort of cycling pilgrim's paradise, and that I was crying with joy perhaps, or relief at leaving Belgium, or all of the above, but it turned out to be merely prophetic sorrow at the trials and tribulations that awaited me there.

Chapter 8: "We killed God forty years ago"

In France everyone appeared to be in the permanent grip of a fit of road rage, as if this was just part of everyday experience, like hunger or tiredness. I saw angry Frenchmen jumping out of their cars to shake their fists at other motorists. I saw dozens of near-crashes. I was myself constantly on the receiving end of hooting, yelling and gesticulations. I couldn't understand what they were yelling, but I was pretty sure it wasn't: "We think you are a very sexy middle-aged woman in those baggy shorts."

In France I was to witness the most ill-tempered driving of the various countries I passed through on my way to Greece. So bad was it, it felt as I was taking my life in my hands every time I set off along a French road. Where these were narrow I learned to leap off my bicycle and flatten myself against a hedge or a wall at the first hint of an approaching vehicle. To say it was stressful would be understating the case.

The French-Belgian border region was also my first introduction to real hills and I wasn't very good at hills. Hills meant getting off the bike and walking, so it took much longer than it should have to get to my first French town, a place called Longwy, which really wasn't far at all. In Longwy I tried to find an inexpensive hotel for the night, for there was no campsite.

The only inexpensive hotel was called "Mr Bed," but the man at the reception desk looked down his nose at me and informed me there were none available. The carpark was deserted and I could see no reason why a large, budget hotel in Longwy should have no available bed in early spring, especially as there wasn't another soul to be seen.

I could only conclude the unavailability of a bed in Mr Bed's establishment had something to do with the odour that had come from a day's walking beside a bicycle, the fact that I did not have a reservation, and the perhaps understandable aversion felt by the receptionist to a smelly cyclist who did not speak French.

Exhausted, tearful, and in daylight that was fading fast, I had to tackle a further fifteen or so kilometers over yet more hills to the nearest campsite, where perhaps they wouldn't be so particular about scruffy, odiferous cyclists.

It became a desperate race to reach the camping ground before darkness fell completely. With no light on my bicycle and a growing and justified mistrust of French drivers, it would have been silly to be out and about on a bicycle after dark.

The campsite, which was advertised as a farm, turned out to be someone's back garden in a village near Languyon. The facilities were basic to say the least. I was the only camper and I interrupted the family at dinner. Monsieur was very surprised to find himself with a customer, and jerked a thumb in the direction of the back garden before returning to his evening meal.

"Please not to eat the cats," he said.

I assured him I had no intention of eating the cats and, after setting up the tent, opened a tin of sardines for my dinner, which was all I had, along with half a loaf of bread.

Seven starving cats emerged out of the gloom. It seemed that not only was I not to feed them, but that nobody ever fed them. I had never seen cats in such terrible condition before, and I hope I never do so again. It was disgusting. Not even in Greece was I to see such pitiful creatures, and Greece does not have a reputation for being particularly concerned about the welfare of cats. The seven wraiths ate all of my sardines and bread, and I went to bed hungry. It pains me to remember them, it pains me to record it.

I left with the dawn the next morning, because I could not bear to look upon the suffering of those poor creatures one more second. It was as much as I could do to be civil to the householder's wife when I paid my bill for the privilege of spending the night in cat-auschwitz.

It was a tough day's cycling: the nearest campsite was in Verdun, some 50km to the south. For the seasoned cyclist 50km is nothing at all, they do more than twice that in a day without staining their lycra, but for the incompetent cyclist, 50km was a serious day's work. But the landscape of Lorraine in North East France was a beautiful unfolding of gentle hills, trees and farmland, and the campsite in Verdun, when I finally arrived, was comfortable and clean.

Verdun was an interesting place, with a violent and turbulent history, derived, as history usually is, from its geographical location. The city, and the area around it, had for centuries been a battlefield. Lying close to the oft-disputed German border, the city was got up like a giant war memorial. Everywhere were monuments, plaques and statues in honour of the glorious sons or daughters of France who had given their lives for the motherland. The patriotism generated by such a history, and by so many tangible reminders of wars past, was tangible. It was the sort of place old men with distant memories and detailed knowledge of historical battles like to visit. It also had the atmosphere of places that have seen a lot of bloodshed, which is impossible to describe, except perhaps as a kind of melancholy.

On one of my nights in Verdun I treated myself to dinner in a café on the banks of the river Meuse, which was to be my companion for some days to come, as it wound its way south, taking me in the general direction of Greece. It was a majestic river, slow moving and in spite of its peculiar milky green colour that looked less than clean, surprisingly attractive.

Eating out was a rare treat; that €15 daily budget didn't really stretch to such indulgences, and so I wandered happily around the café and restaurant-lined promenade along the banks of the river, relishing the task of choosing somewhere to eat, instead of warming a tin of something unexciting on my tiny oil primus.

It was a beautiful evening with the late sun warming the pastel stones of the ancient buildings on the other side of the river. I sat for hours watching the Meuse and the world go by. In France, watching the world go by usually meant watching packs of black-clad motorcyclists go by. Everywhere I went there were packs of black-clad motorcyclists. It was an extraordinary phenomenon: they never went anywhere singly, and they never wore any colour other than black.

They had the most peculiar attitude to cyclists, too. Never once was I overtaken by a black pack of motorcyclists without being subjected to jeers, shouts, and rude hand gestures. It was hard not to be affected by it, for I came in peace, not war.

I have to confess to being a little disappointed in France. I'd been before, on that youthful trip mentioned previously, but that had been to different parts of France. I'd been to Provence, and later to Paris, and had found both places magical, but this part of France had a darkness about it. Perhaps it was the history. Perhaps centuries effectively constituting the front line, forced to repel endless attempted invasions, had made the people a little aggressive. Perhaps the attitude of the black packs was some sort of Darwinist adaption to a history of warfare. Or perhaps there was another cause entirely: religion or the lack of it.

[Warning: Short religious rant follows.]

I have always been interested in the sociology of religion, and the area of France that I was riding through provided plenty of food for thought in this matter. I was inclined to attribute the aggressive behavior of the black packs to the widespread decline of religion in this part of France, for I am of the admittedly controversial opinion that the religiosity of a region has a direct bearing on the behavior of its residents. And here the decline in religion was strikingly apparent everywhere in the advanced decay of the religious buildings and monuments.

In Britain, where the majority of people aren't particularly religious anymore either, the churches nevertheless tend to be in reasonably good repair. In rural Greece, when I finally got there, and which is still very religious, the churches were always the best-kept buildings in any village. No matter how poor or run down everything else was, the church would shine like a well-polished jewel in the midst of it all.

But in this part of France the churches were in a terrible state. It was as if religion had declined more dramatically in that country than anywhere else, and as if they were saying, we aren't even going to pretend we give a shit by keeping up appearances.

On the road to St Mihiel, I saw an old wood and iron crucifix standing at the side of the road. It was some ten feet tall and intricately wrought. Someone had cared enough to create it and erect it there, a gift to the roadside in the days when such things still meant something. But now it was worn and uncared for and it made me think of a thermometer, standing up straight, and declaring the spiritual temperature of the area.

In the church of St Mihiel in the town of the same name, the once beautiful Corinthian columns supporting the arches of the nave were worn, with the fluting crumbling and blunted. High on the walls at the rear of the nave a magnificent Renaissance-style painting was torn and darkened with the grime of centuries and in a state now well beyond repair, which seemed like a double desecration really, of both art and religion.

I asked the lady in the tourist information office why this was so. She shrugged. "We do what we can in France," she said, "but there are so many churches, and there is only so much we can do."

Ironically this was the area that also gave birth to one of the most passionate and dramatic figures in the history of Christianity. For I'd found myself, quite by chance, in the land of Jeanne d'Arc. And there were no tourists, not one, or if there were they were keeping a low profile. It was early in the season, yes, but even so, surely tourists would flock to the birthplace of Joan of Arc right round the year? There'd be heaps of church-based package tours wouldn't there?

"Oh, people don't come here because of Jeanne d'Arc anymore," a local told me. "They come because of the natural beauty, if they come at all."

Jeanne was born, baptized and raised in the village of Domremy, where I now found myself. Pious from childhood, she claimed to hear the voices of saints and angels. At the age of 14 she announced that her voices had commanded her to lead France against the English and because it was the fifteenth century, when all things were still possible, they took her seriously instead of prescribing medication. So began Jeanne's astonishing journey that included audiences with Charles II, marches through wild countryside with companies of soldiers, armed battles, victories and defeats, and, ultimately, burning at the stake at the hands of fanatical and spiteful inquisitors, which couldn't have been a pleasant way to die, whichever way you look at it.

I spent the night at a bed-and-breakfast between Vaulcouleurs and Domremy, where the son of the family, an expert in something called "auto organization," had plenty of strong views on religion, and was more than happy to share them. He'd earned his doctorate looking at ants, watching them do their tunneling and nest-building and from this he had reached the conclusion that ants were exceedingly rational, but also exceedingly unreflective.

"They build efficient and complex nests with excellent ventilation, without the slightest understanding of what it is that they are doing," he said.

He then made a bit of a leap, and applied the insights of ant organization to the complexity of human societies. It was not difficult to see where this line of thinking was headed.

"Seeing the world through the spectacles of auto-organization reduces all activity, including that of the human, to an evolutionary drive to efficiency," he said. And in his view, the decay of France's churches was just another positive indicator that France was organizing itself along rational lines.

"There is no room for God in such a world. We killed God twenty, or perhaps forty years ago," he said, as if this was something to be proud of.

Leaving Jeanne d'Arc country, I started gearing up to do some cheating on a grand scale, because there were problems with cycling in France, and they were getting worse.

The most pressing of these was called the Alps, and there was no getting round them. I'd have to go over them. I'd now had plenty of opportunity to test out my abilities as a cyclist, and so limited were they, I knew I wouldn't be cycling the Alps, I'd be walking the Alps, and there was no way I was going to do that.

There were problems also with campsites. While France may have had more campsites than any other country in Europe, they tended to be clustered in popular places, in Provence and so on. In this quiet corner of the north east, the campsites were too far apart for daily camp-site-hopping and I was spending far too much money on rooms.

Then there were problems with the language. Aside from the biology lecturer and one or two other tourist-information folk, no-one spoke English, and I was feeling an increasing sense of linguistic isolation. I'd taken a ridiculously optimistic three week crash course in French before I'd left, one of those courses that says you'll be fluent in no time, but all it had given me was a tiny French vocabulary irrelevant to my present needs. I knew how to order a meal in a restaurant, ask the way to the Eiffel Tower, or arrange to meet someone at the Louvre.

Now, some years later, and twelve months into a decent online course, I have realized it takes years, not months or weeks, to acquire an adequate grasp of a language as difficult as French. It takes more than three weeks just to master the subjunctive, for heaven's sake, assuming you even manage to figure out what it is in the first place.

Somehow I scraped by in France with a few phrases, some gesticulation, but mostly by avoiding all forms of human interaction requiring speech. But the loneliness that attended the inability to communicate heightened my desire to reach Greece as quickly as possible. For at that point I was still laboring under the illusion that I could speak a bit of Greek. There's something to be said for illusions: they do protect us from facing the unpleasant realities to come, before it's absolutely necessary to do so.

And lastly there were those motorists and motorcyclists already mentioned, furnishing what was perhaps the most compelling reason to leave France. I would never get used to cycling in France; it was just too much of an ordeal. I cannot speak for other regions of France; it may be different in those, but the terrifying speed and the rudeness of French motorists in north-east France made that overnight train to Nice simply irresistible.

What I didn't know was that in Nice things were going to get a lot worse, making my present problems seem really rather trivial. For all things considered, my midlife crisis was going rather well. I hadn't overspent too badly; I was writing articles; I had a little proofreading work coming in; I was broadening my horizons; and I was healthier than I'd been in years. On the whole life was about as good as it gets.

I knew before I got there that I wasn't going to like Nice. Bicycles and cities don't go together, and I was accompanied by a bicycle. There were logistical problems: I couldn't leave the thing unattended and fully loaded if I needed to nip into a shop to buy something, for example. And then there were the hazards of sharing roads choked with too many vehicles with the capacity and sometimes the will to kill me. There was also something unspeakably lonely about cycling in a city. I never once felt lonely in the countryside — it was only when was surrounded by people and buildings and honking vehicles that I felt a great aching loneliness.

The architecture of Nice was very grand, all in a wonderful mustardy-pink stone, but alongside that there was plenty to repel, for Nice was a city with plenty of poverty and suffering. Once out and about in it, I saw beggars and tramps everywhere, with bodies scattered about, prone on the pavement, in varying stages of alcoholic or drugged stupor.

After a couple of hours in Nice I could have done with an alcoholic or drugged stupor myself. I had found an internet café to transfer funds from one of my three internet banking accounts to my ATM card, which was running low, and it had all gone very badly.

Before leaving New Zealand, I had split my money over three accounts, wisely I thought, in order to protect against loss of one or other card, or some similar unforeseen disaster. One account held considerably more than the other two, almost half my money, and of course Murphy's law now came into operation. For it was this account that suddenly developed a chronic and seemingly unsolvable problem, a discovery that was accompanied by the kind of panic attack that includes palpitations and sweating.

The nature of the problem was complicated, and I am still not sure I fully understand it. Neteller, the bank in question, had been affected by legislative changes in the United States governing the transfer of money to and from internet banks. The legislation had to do with the online gaming industry, recently declared illegal in that country. And because Neteller had connections with the poker industry, everybody's funds had been frozen, unless residency outside the USA could be established. Because I was now officially a resident of Nowhere in Particular, overnight it had become impossible to access a single penny.

I still owned the money in theory, but theoretical money was no use at all. Trembling with panic I contacted the online 'help' chat desk, which was very busy because Neteller had ruined thousands of other lives in one stroke, and everyone wanted to have a chat about it. After a long wait, while the internet meter ticked away at exorbitant city rates, someone appeared online.

"The only way to access your funds is by ordering a cheque," he or she typed in answer to my panicked question.

"I am travelling," I typed back. "I can't order a cheque, because I don't have a mailing address. Surely there must be another way?"

"The only way to access your funds is by ordering a cheque. Now is there anything else I can help you with today? Thank you for banking with Neteller."

There is nothing quite like being stuck in a foreign city and discovering that you have lost access to more than half your funds. And it's not as if I had a lot of them in the first place. The whole aspect of the place changed in a twinkling. Mustardy pink became the colour of nightmares. There was now nothing nice about Nice.

The original plan had been to cycle from Nice to Arles, a bit of a detour, but Van Gogh had lived there once, and I had thought it would be lovely to spend a few days near the Provencal town where the great man had gone mad, cycling through the countryside he'd painted, just as I'd done in Holland.

But that was now out of the question. The south of France would have been expensive even on my previous tight budget of €15 a day. But now that had been cut in half to just €7.50, I wouldn't even be able to afford campsite fees in Provence, let alone food and drink.

The solution was obvious. Greece. I'd head for Greece as fast as possible. Everything would be cheaper and better in Greece, for was it not the promised land?

The only glimmer of light in that terrible dark day was a proofreading assignment from my previous employer. So I sat in the overpriced internet café for a few hours trying to concentrate on grammar and sentence construction, which was not easy with a churning stomach, hot and cold sweats, palpitations, and the prospect of imminent starvation in a foreign land. But I persevered and sent the document on its way through cyberspace. At least there would be a little money coming in soon.

There was also an email from Polly, wanting to know how long it might be before she could come and join me. Should she bring the blue dress as well as the green dress, or should she get rid of the blue dress? What did I think? And would there be any need for evening gowns in Greece? She was going through her wardrobe getting rid of things she didn't think would be suitable for her new life in Greece. It was looking like Polly had made up her mind to come, and when Polly had made up her mind to something, no power in heaven or on earth would stop her.

What had I done? What had I done?

I spent the rest of the morning hanging about the station with the drunks and drug addicts, trying to make sense of the limited options available to me. The furthest I could go with my bicycle by train was a place called Ventimiglia, just across the border into Italy, in fact. From there I would have to hop from one painfully slow regional train to another.

To make matters worse, no-one in Nice's railway station was willing or able to help me figure out what to do when I got to Italy.

"You will have to ask how to get across Italy in Ventimiglia," the surly ticket seller said.

The train to Ventimiglia was due to leave from the furthest platform, which involved the now regrettably familiar procedure of unloading it, lugging the panniers down the long steep stairs into the bowels of the earth, going back for the bicycle, and doing the same in reverse the other end, while the gentlemen of Nice propped themselves up against the station walls, looking cool.

Perhaps it was naïve and old fashioned of me to cling to the lingering belief that it is a good thing for big strong men to assist a woman who is clearly struggling. There were places in the world where this still happened, a charming custom from a bygone era that really shouldn't be allowed to fall into complete disuse.

The train to Ventimiglia passed through Monte Carlo, affording fleeting glimpses of the dwellings of the rich and the famous, with their lives that were so very far removed from mine, and it was difficult to repress pangs of a most ignoble envy. Then it was across the border into Italy, where unfolded the events already chronicled in Chapter 1, in which I ended up with an unknown number of broken ribs and a hangover.

Chapter 9: "Even the Fish are Happy Here"

It was the morning after the night before. I awoke in the seedy Italian station hotel to a searing pain in my ribcage. It felt as if I had broken not one, but all of them. Every movement was torture and it took forever to pack my panniers and heave them into the antiquated hotel elevator and down to the lobby, where my bicycle awaited after its night in a cupboard under the stairs. Then there was the searing pain in my head from the cheap Italian plonk I'd used as a painkiller, which had not been the cleverest idea.

Cycling was still possible, just unspeakably painful, and if I moved suddenly the pain was instantly elevated from awful to unbearable in a series of super intense white hot stabs. Cycling may look like an activity performed by the lower half of the body, but there's a surprising amount of movement that goes on in the upper half too, leading to plenty of white hot stabs in the side.

So it was very gingerly that I pedaled through the early morning traffic and back to the ferry terminal. My ferry didn't leave till late afternoon, but sightseeing in Ancona, assuming there were any sights to be seen, and I'll never know but I somehow doubt it, was out of the question.

The ferry terminal had come to life and was thronged with passengers, mountains of luggage everywhere, and everyone in a good mood, which was not surprising considering they were all leaving Italy for Greece. And it was surely a good omen that the ticket seller who sold me my passage to Igoumenitsa on the appropriately named *Hellenic Spirit* was not in the least surly.

I found a bench where I sat all day, trying not to move, watching people and boats coming and going. At last it was time to board and I wheeled the bicycle into the car deck and tied it to the wall to stop it falling over. I unhitched one of the panniers and took it upstairs with me; the one containing the oldest laptop in the world, for I was in the habit of guarding it as if it was important.

Thanks to the Financial Disaster, I was travelling deck class. Deck class on a drafty overnight ferry wouldn't have been a lot of fun at the best of times, and with an unspecified number of broken ribs, this did not count as the best of times.

Passengers travelling deck class had the use of a large and drafty lounge, furnished with rows of chairs called aeroplane seats, which merely meant they had two positions: bolt upright and almost bolt upright.

Each seat was separated by an armrest of the immovable variety, effectively preventing anyone from stretching out in anything approaching comfort, whether the ferry was empty or full, and in this case it was almost empty. The only chance of stretching out was on the floor.

My fellow travellers, knowing about this in advance, had come equipped with sleeping bags, pillows and mattresses. I too had come equipped with such things: I had a sleeping bag, a foam bedroll, and clothing I could roll up into a pillow, the way I did in my tent.

But these indispensable aids to comfort were still on the bicycle that was tied to the wall in the car deck. I had had an entire day sitting in the ferry terminal in Ancona doing absolutely nothing at all to sort all this out in advance, but in my pain-befuddled state, I'd not given it any thought. I now had with me everything that was useless, and nothing at all that was useful.

For there was now a man guarding the car deck against anyone with a will to steal the panniers containing the various useful things that would have reduced the misery of the voyage. And not only was he guarding them against potential thieves, he was also guarding them against me. No amount of begging or pleading would persuade him to allow me to fetch any of them.

The other comfort that was denied me on that ferry trip to Greece was the comfort of my illusions. For the extent to which I'd fooled myself into thinking I knew enough Greek to get by had now dawned on me. For the past two months, with every embarrassing or difficult linguistic exchange, I'd consoled myself with the thought that at least when I got to Greece I'd be able to make myself understood.

There was a television set in the corner of the lounge running non-stop news in Greek and I understood not a single word of it. There were some potentially mitigating factors here, because Greek television was a phenomenon of singular uniqueness. The screen was divided into six rectangles, and in each rectangle there was the head of a person, representing some or other point of view, although I had no idea what it was, because I had just discovered I didn't speak Greek. It was clear at least that they were opposing views, because everyone was shouting, and they were all shouting at once. The person who shouted the loudest was the one who got heard, which is probably a universal truth as well as a particular truth about Greek television.

Any small sop of comfort I might have been tempted to offer myself that I could not understand what they were saying because they were all shouting was also speedily banished, for there were real live Greeks all around me, and I couldn't understand a word they were saying either.

So I was off to live in a country where I didn't speak the language after all. It was the perfect time, really, for another crisis within the greater crisis. These crises were now following one another in quick succession. What was I doing? What had I done? I was just weeks away from starvation, I was injured in a way that made cycling impossible, at least till my ribcage had mended, and there was no going back.

The sole comfort to be had that night was in the form of a group of students sharing my corner of the lounge. They were from the University of Johannina, on their way home from a conference in Switzerland, and they were friendly and polite, unlike the youths of some other countries I could mention.

I got talking to Nikkos, who was some years into a PhD in plant physiology. This meant he got to spend a lot of time watching trees grow and analyzing the differences between deciduous, semi-deciduous and non deciduous forests. It sounded a very pleasant way to earn a PhD, much more so than mine, which had involved ten years looking at church doctrine and trying to figure out what was wrong with it. No contest, really.

Nikkos was bitter about the education system in Greece. "The problem," he said, "is that the entrance exam into university is more difficult than the degree itself. So when you start your studies, it feels like you are going backwards, and it's really boring. You know all this stuff already. That is why I went on to further study, to compensate for the regression, and to make it all feel worthwhile."

Now, years of study later, instead of it all feeling worthwhile, he was growing heartily sick of being an impoverished doctoral student and I could relate to that. It was even worse for him than it had been for me, because doctoral students in Greece were expected to work as tutors, and they didn't get paid for it. "Unless you have a wealthy family it is all very difficult," he said.

Nikkos gave me a painkiller for my ribs, which was very kind of him, and I settled down to try and sleep on the hard carpet. People were coming and going all through the night, and each time the doors opened a fresh blast of cold air whistled through the lounge, making sleep impossible.

But in the morning, although a long time coming, it was easy to forget the discomfort of the night, for Albania was now on our left, and then it was Greece, with Corfu on the right. There was a mounting sense of excitement on board, as passengers thronged the decks to watch the land masses slip past. Greeks, it seemed, liked Greece a lot, and couldn't wait to get back there. I too was swept up in the excitement of being on a boat heading somewhere beautiful.

The ferry swung slowly into the harbour of Igoumenitsa, which looked lovely from a distance, with the town behind glowing in the early morning sunshine. Up close it wasn't quite so lovely; it was a little seedy and chaotic, but it was Greece and could thus be forgiven everything.

Not many people disembarked in Igoumenitsa, because there wasn't much reason to do so. Most were travelling on to Patras, some five hours further south, because that was within easy reach of Athens and some of the more popular tourist destinations.

But I wanted a taste of remote rural Greece, and Igoumenitsa was about as remote and rural as it got, so I wheeled my bicycle across the nearly deserted ferry terminal, and took the hilly road to the south where at once the Greekness of Greece hit me.

I had waited two decades to return to this country I'd visited in my early twenties, and not even the pain in my side could stop my heart from overflowing with joy. It was all just as I remembered it—the rugged landscape, the cloudless sky, the sounds of nature singing: cicadas, birds, and everywhere the herds of goats with their tinkling bells.

The wild flowers were still in bloom and the hills were a riot of red, purple, yellow and pink. It was glorious. I had arrived in the promised land, and I couldn't have been happier.

The road from Igoumenitsa to the south was narrow and potholed, and it weaved like a snake over the natural obstacles of the landscape. It was, in short, a dangerous road, something attested to by the little roadside shrines erected on every bend. These were elaborate and decorative constructions, usually in the shape of miniature churches.

They contained icons, oil, water and candles, and there was usually a photograph of the young man — as often as not it was a young man — who'd gone flying over a cliff in a burst of excessive testosterone-induced speed.

I was to cycle past many a rural cottage industry, the shrines set out in rows in the sun, waiting for the next unfortunate grieving family to come along. It was a thriving business, this industry in roadside shrines, and if the Greeks ever got their driving together, a great many people would have gone out of business.

But that was unlikely with 13.8 deaths per 100 000 people caused by bad driving. For purposes of comparison, in the United Kingdom bad driving results in a much more respectable 4.8 deaths per 100 000.

Mindful of the dangers, and having no wish to augment the statistics, I cycled very circumspectly to my destination, a campsite near the village of Plataria, some ten kilometers south of Igoumenitsa.

In doing so I was soon made aware of another significant national characteristic of Greek motorists. Yes, they drove like lunatics at speeds better suited to German autobahns than narrow mountain passes, but they did so in great good humour.

In France and Italy I'd been hooted at constantly, and this accompanied by clenched fists, the finger, the V sign, and I'm not talking about V for Victory. In Greece I was hooted at constantly also, but it was a different kind of hooting. It was friendly hooting, accompanied by waves and smiles and shouts of encouragement, eyes off the road, wild swerving, and a carefree disregard for the 100 foot ravine just ahead with the very real attendant possibility of ending up immortalized in a roadside shrine alongside cousin Giorgos.

The camping ground, my first in Greece, was a delight, which was just as well, since I would be stuck there until my ribs healed. I wasn't sure how long this would take, because I'd not sought the wisdom of a medical man (or woman). This was in part because of the Financial Disaster, and in part because I didn't have medical insurance (people who travel without maps tend to be the same people who don't have medical insurance), but only in part.

The main reason was because I was one of those people who always knew better than any doctor when it came to my own body. I *knew* I had cracked or broken one or more ribs. I didn't need a doctor and expensive x-rays to confirm that. The only benefit in seeking confirmation would be to discover just how many, and how badly. I also knew there wasn't a lot you could do about broken and cracked ribs. The only thing I didn't know was how long it would be before they mended, and there didn't seem any particular advantage in knowing that either.

The campsite was run by a youngish man who wore very tight jeans, a very tight t-shirt and walked with a swagger. With his slicked back hair and his dazzling white smile, he was like a caricature of the Mediterranean lover. He showed me a place just meters away from the sea where I could pitch my tent, and as we stood there, admiring the view, I could see fish leaping in the bay, dozens of them. He pointed to them and said,

"Welcome to Greece. See, even the fish are happy here."

Pitching tent was agony. I had not realized before the accident what a lot of stretching, bending and twisting is involved in the business of pitching a tent. But it was an idyllic spot—the waters of the Adriatic were sparkling, and at all times those fish could be seen jumping for joy. At night the wind in the hills sounded like choirs singing, and that's not just a figure of speech, it really did.

I was in Greece, and I was in no wise disappointed. So often in my life dreams had turned to dust the moment they became real, but for once this was not the case. Greece was just as wonderful and beautiful as I remembered it, and it was still a spiritual place, a place where they'd not got round to killing God yet, and God knows, there's few enough of those places left on earth.

I took advantage of my immobilization to start writing in earnest. When I left New Zealand in search of the sun, and in search of a very different life, but with very little money, I knew I was taking a massive risk.

But I backed myself. I could string sentences together in a passable fashion; I had an adequate eye for a story. Some years spent as a salaried journalist back in my early twenties had taught me a thing or two. I thought it likely that my adventure would yield sufficient raw material for articles. And then there were my proofreading skills. If writing failed, I could always fall back on those.

I had reckoned, I suppose, without Reality.

My first article, about the Bangkok sapphire scam, was accepted at once. It was published at once, too. I was given a three quarter page spread, with an enormous byline, in Wellington's Dominion Post. Friends and acquaintances wrote to congratulate me. My editorial contact sent a scan of the article along with a nicely worded thank you note.

I was delighted, exhilarated, exonerated. That would silence those Doubting Thomases once and for all. It was indeed possible to make a living as a writer while travelling. I think I even treated myself to dinner in a Real Restaurant, instead of cooking my sparse daily rations on the little spirit stove I carried in my bicycle panniers. I did not know at that point there's many a slip twixt publication and payment.

I inquired about payment nonchalantly. How is payment effected for freelance articles? I tried not sound too interested in the money side of things. I did not want my new editorial contact to think I was *only in it for the money....*

Send me your contact details, she replied, bank details, address and so on, and I will pass them on to our accounts department for payment. No sum was mentioned, and it seemed vulgar to inquire further. I tend to think, retrospectively, that no sum was mentioned because my contact was too embarrassed to name the paltry sum I would eventually receive.

And I use the word eventually with reason. Weeks went by, whole countries went by, and I heard nothing. I was forced to send a further, somewhat plaintive email to my editorial contact. To her credit she must have put the screws on Accounts Payable, because by return email I received a detailed message from Julie in Accounts Payable. Julie had provided for my entertainment a series of informative pamphlets and forms. The forms were to be completed and returned by fax, and the pamphlets described all the hoops I was going to have to jump through in order to receive payment.

Julie in Accounts Payable had obviously never been to Plataria, or if she had, she and the powers to whom she answered didn't give a toss how difficult it was to find internet/faxing facilities there that were sophisticated enough to meet the accounting requirements of Fairfax Media. (Fairfax Media is the publishing consortium that owns the Dominion Post and far too many other New Zealand publications.)

It took me the best part of a morning and cost me the best part of €20 to fulfill the demands of Fairfax Media for proof of this and that, to fill in Inland Revenue forms, and to find somewhere to fax the whole lot back.

The process, Julie in Accounts Payable informed me, also required that I obtain a 'purchase order' from the person who had commissioned the article, and that, once my details had been 'approved,' I should submit an invoice. There were detailed instructions concerning the formatting of said invoice.

I emailed back saying my article had been published weeks ago, was not 'commissioned' for some future date, and could they please pay me accordingly.

There was silence for some weeks. At last I was forced to humble myself again, and write to my editorial contact. I thought to include a few further articles in the email. She took a fancy to one of them, and so things happened more quickly after that. I received, by return email, a "purchase order" for the original article. And so the whole expensive process continued. I had to spend more time, and more money, in an over-priced Greek internet café, devising and sending the pointless invoice, making sure I quoted, as requested, the purchase order number.Eventually, and after an interval of several months, I received in my bank account the princely sum of $150. And this was New Zealand dollars, not American.

Once I subtracted the money I had spent on getting it published, internet time, and, more to the point, the money I had spent trying to get paid, the net profit would amount to no more than $100. It had taken me three days to write the article, and at least another day wasted chasing Julie in Accounts. That worked out as a daily wage of $25.

Similar woes and difficulties dogged subsequent articles, and those were the success stories. How much more depressing were the failures, for I discovered another unpleasant fact about newspaper and magazine editors: if they weren't interested they didn't bother to reply. Because I had been led to believe it was wrong to submit the same article to multiple destinations, the silence was very difficult to manage. At what point should I give up on publication A, assume silence meant no, and send the article to publication B? I never managed to work that one out. Now, of course, I'd send everything everywhere simultaneously. But that was then, and I was still playing by some book that had long since gone out of print.

With the financial situation so dire, I started looking at those happy fish leaping in the waters of the bay in a new light. I would take up fishing, I decided. I'd sit on a rock at the water's edge, and coax the fish of Plataria Bay into my frying pan.

This was not the first time I had wanted to try fishing. When I was nine, my brothers and father went off on a week-long boys-only fishing trip and because fishing sounded fun, had desperately wanted to go with them. But I was left behind with Polly instead, who had just three words to say on the subject: "Girls don't fish."

The time now seemed perfect to catch two fish with one hook, so to speak. I'd

right what was clearly an historical injustice, and ease my financial problems at the same time. But girls didn't fish in Greece either, not if the reaction of the man in the fishing tackle shop was any indication. He fell about laughing once we'd got through the usual preliminaries.

The usual preliminaries followed a pattern that seldom varied and started with the question: "Are you German?" It took a while to realize the significance of this question, and just why the reply "No, I am from New Zealand" had such a powerful and positive effect.

The Second World War and the German occupation lay at the bottom of it, because the Germans hadn't been particularly gentlemanly when they'd overrun Greece in the 1940s. In some parts of the country the animus towards Germans was particularly strong, especially among the older members of the population, because these were areas that had seen plenty of action and plenty of tragedy.

The area I was in was one of those. There had been some particularly horrible massacres up there in the mountainous north. I wasn't too far from a village called Mousiotitsa, where, in 1945, German SS troops executed 153 villagers because of the participation of some in resistance activities. They didn't stop at killing the men; women and children were also slaughtered, and the Greek people have long memories.

In this matter I had an unexpected advantage. For it was New Zealand soldiers who fought on the side of the Greeks, and not a few died alongside them. The Greeks, it turned out, had long memories for good as well as ill.

And while I wasn't a New Zealander by birth, having lived there more than twenty years I considered myself one. I certainly didn't feel British, which is what my passport said I was, and neither did I feel South African, which is where I was born. I'd adopted New Zealand as my homeland, I had a New Zealand accent, and so that's where I said I was from.

If I'd announced I was an angel from heaven above the people of Greece couldn't have been more welcoming. This unexpected and by no means unwelcome discovery was confirmed by a New Zealand couple I met further south. They were travelling around in a campervan and the man was wearing a T shirt with the words 'Good Bastards' written on it in large black letters.

In New Zealand the phrase, "He's a Good Bastard," is probably the highest accolade that can be paid a man, although this subtle nuance was no doubt lost on the good people of Greece. The Good Bastard and his wife told me of a night they had camped in an olive grove somewhere between Patras and Olympia. The New Zealand flag and the Kiwi emblem hung from cycle racks at the rear of their van, and their country of origin was thus not difficult to fathom.

After a while a little old lady appeared out of nowhere, dressed all in black, as little old ladies in Greece tend to be, bearing an overflowing basket of fruit and vegetables. She didn't speak a word of English and the Good Bastards didn't speak a word of Greek, but she pressed her gift upon them. Bewildered by this unsolicited kindness, they made her a cup of coffee and the three of them then sat for an hour or so beneath the olives, unable to communicate. It didn't stop the little old lady rambling on in Greek and having a little cry every now and then. The Good Bastards just smiled and nodded uncomprehendingly.

The mystery was cleared up next morning when the lady's grandson appeared and he did speak English. A New Zealand solder, he said, had saved the life of his grandmother's husband during World War II.

The Good Bastards had another story about their personal experience of Greek-German-New Zealand relations. They'd parked their campervan on private land near a beach, taking a chance the landowner would turn a blind eye to their trespass. Shortly afterwards a large and shiny German campervan pulled up also.

Within minutes the landowner appeared, waving his arms, yelling angrily, and making it quite plain that the Germans were to *raus*, and they were to *raus* immediately. The Good Bastards meekly started packing up their gear also, but the landowner turned to them and said, "No, not you, you may stay as long as you like…"

I had similar experiences as I made my way south, although not quite as dramatic as those of the Good Bastards. High in the hills in the province of Messinia, for example, I met a very old man on an equally ancient motorcycle who jumped off and embraced me as soon as I told him I was from New Zealand. Very near here, he told me, a small group of New Zealand soldiers held back the advancing Germans.

"It's not forgotten, you know," the Good Bastard said. "The Greek people will never forget."

In one of those ironic twists of history, the Germans are now back in Greece in numbers, invading and occupying again, but this time they come in peace, and bring wads of Euro dollars with them. And whenever I asked outright how the one-time enemy was viewed in Greece, time and again I heard the same response: "We have forgiven the Germans." I was not at all convinced of that, because everything I saw and experienced suggested the opposite: that deep down, the Germans were anything but forgiven.

"Are you German?" asked the man in the fishing tackle shop, his expression brightening when I assured him I was not. He asked what I wanted, and once he'd stopped laughing, he sorted me out with some line, some hooks, and some small metal things he called double-barreled swivels.

I had no idea what to do with them, so he showed me how it all worked: how to attach hooks, swivels and the round metal things to a piece of fishing line. A few dexterous twists later — his not mine — and I had the basic equipment needed for fishing.

"All you need now is bait," he said, producing a cardboard box from beneath the counter and opening it for inspection. I had expected it to contain something unexceptionable, like little chunks of dried fish.

I had not expected to see a writhing mass of worms, very much alive, each about two inches long. I recoiled in horror. I had not thought about this aspect of fishing, and did not think I would be capable of touching one, let along impaling it on a hook.

"Don't you have something else I can use?" I asked. "Something that's not alive?"

He was now crying he was laughing so much. But he put the box away and produced another container, this time from the refrigerator. The worms in this box were a lot smaller, and not nearly so disgusting, but as bait, not so effective either, he told me.

"Not so good," he said, "but better than dead bait."

That was all very well, but they were still alive and they were still worms. There was no getting away from that. Dead bait sounded much more my style.

"But the fish do not like dead bait," he said, wiping the tears from his cheeks. "It does not tempt them." And so I capitulated, and gingerly accepted the loathsome box of small live and decidedly untempting worms. He stood in the doorway and waved, still laughing, as I cycled off with my purchases.

The fish were leaping in the bay. They were there by the hundred, but first I had to impale a couple of live worms on a fishing hook. I shall not dwell upon the many times my hand hovered over that box with its horrible cargo and withdrew, but finally I managed it.

When the hooks were baited with the unfortunate worms that I'd impaled, it was time to try casting my line. I had seen the Greek men do it—they would swung the line around their head like a lasso and then let fly, and the baited hook would sail effortlessly some 50 meters out to sea, before plopping in at the appointed spot.

I shall not dwell upon the length of time it took to achieve a casting of more than a meter, or even a casting that did not get caught in the bushes behind me, I finally managed a plop—some 40 meters short of the appointed spot—but at least it was in the water.

My hopes were high. The fish were leaping and cavorting and soon they would be leaping into my frying pan. Alas it didn't take too many hours to realize the fish had no intention of becoming dinner, because the fish in Greece were not stupid. They could see perfectly well that the worm was attached to a hook. Perhaps I should have bought the larger worms after all. I caught two things that day—a leaf and a stone—and it was beans as usual for dinner.

After a few days in Plataria, and when I was feeling a bit better, I took a walk into the nearby hills and at the top of a rough path stumbled on a tiny chapel in a flowery garden, for in Greece there were at least as many chapels per capita as there were cars. Sitting in the garden, dressed in full clerical garb, and smoking a cigarette, was an elderly Greek Orthodox priest, for the anti-smoking evangelists have made little headway in Greece and everybody smokes like chimneys, even the men of God.

He seemed pleased to see me there and we got talking. "Hello," he said. "My name is Papas Efklidis. Are you German?"

The chapel, which was lovely, was dedicated to a saint called Friday, and there wasn't an inch of wall that wasn't covered in icons bearing a particularly striking symbol, which was a dish with two eyes in it. I asked him what it meant.

Saint Friday, or Agias Paraskevi as it is in Greek, was born in Rome of Greek parents one Friday around the year 140 AD, he told me. She was very devout, and when her parents died she gave away all her possessions and travelled the countryside preaching, which wasn't the wisest thing to do in a country and a time where Christians were the staple diet of lions. It wasn't too long before she had annoyed enough people to get herself arrested and thrown into prison.

The Emperor, one Antonius Pius, decided to throw her into a vat of boiling oil and tar to teach her a lesson, but because she was on such good terms with the Deity, she was unharmed, and this angered the Emperor greatly. He demanded to know if she'd used a magic trick to protect herself, and to prove she hadn't she threw some of the boiling oil in his face.

Because he wasn't on nearly such good terms with the Deity, Antonius was instantly blinded, and he begged her to intervene and heal him. Not being one to bear a grudge, she obliged, hence the origin of the symbol of the eyes. On the strength of this miracle Antonius Pius decided it would be prudent to cease religious persecution and so he granted freedom to Christians throughout the empire.

They didn't all live happily ever after, though, for after the death of Pius, persecuting Christians was soon back in vogue, and after suffering further unpleasant tortures, Paraskevi was beheaded and not even God could put her back together again. Nowadays, said Papas Efklidis, who clearly believed every word of the story, pilgrims who visit her tomb are cured of their ailments, especially blindness.

"You would like to come to our church service on Sunday in the town?" he asked.

"You will need to wear a skirt," he said, pointing to his own skirted legs.

Then he turned his attention to domestic matters. Like most Greek men, he was interested in my family, and in particular my "andras" – my husband. "Where is your andras?" was usually the next question I was asked after "Are you a German?" The men of Greece seemed to find the answer — that I didn't have one — quite shocking. From this I gathered that even though it was the twenty-first century, it was still something of a scandal to be a woman travelling through Greece alone on a bicycle, unaccompanied by an andras. Women were still generally expected to stay at home, under the protection of said andras, especially in remote rural areas such as this one. "Bravo," said Papas Efklidis, doubtfully, looking more than a little dubious about the propriety of me cycling andras-less through Greece.

So on Sunday morning I cycled down the hill from the campsite to the village of Plataria, wearing a skirt that kept getting entangled in the chain, because bicycles weren't designed for skirts and skirts weren't designed for bicycles. Plataria was a simple fishing port, with a population of around a thousand, a significant proportion of these immigrants from nearby Albania. Restaurants and tavernas lined the harbour and here the old men spent their days drinking coffee, chatting, and playing cards or backgammon.

The village itself was poor, but the church was a place of voluptuous beauty, the largest building in the village — a large neo-Byzantine structure, decorated with colourful murals and liberal quantities of gold leaf. When it came to their churches, it was as if the people of Greece felt the need to compete with nature, and since the natural beauty was itself so spectacular, the care that went into the design and decoration of churches produced an almost supernatural effort.

I was there punctually, at 8.30 am, because that is what Anglicans do, but aside from Papas Efklidis and his young assistant, there was just myself and two wizened old ladies dressed in black. I felt saddened. Such a beautiful church and only five of us had bothered to turn up.

But as time passed, I realized Greek Orthodox church services, like everything else in Greece, were subject to Greek time and Greek ways. Starting time might have been 8.30, but that was just the notional time. People started turning up in dribs and drabs and an hour later they were still coming. They would slip a coin or two into the collection box and then grab a fistful of candles to plant in a gold receptacle that quickly became a festival of lighted candles.

In Greek churches there were proper candles, which you lit with proper matches and that burned with proper flames. Italy, I discovered, had moved on to electric candles. A coin in a slot would cause a fake electric candle to light up and shine for a designated amount of time. Then it would switch off automatically. I am sure there is some important insight into the difference between the two countries buried in there somewhere.

There was a lot of coming and going during Sunday morning worship in Plataria. Folk would jump up wander about kissing icons. I was never tempted to kiss an icon because it seemed a vaguely disgusting thing to do, in light of all the previous decades that the icons had been subjected to kissing.

The choir formed in a disorderly fashion, with old men joining Papas Efklidis' assistant at the singing business as and when they felt like it, and at one point two of the oldest ladies in the congregation went forward and prostrated themselves to kiss the hem of Papa Efklidis gown. I wondered how that worked: was there a roster for hem kissing, or was hem kissing a spontaneous event? It was impossible to tell.

At last it was time for the blessed bread, great chunks of village bread doled out by Papas Efklidis. I noticed he gave extra chunks to the elderly and to the poorer-looking members of his congregation. Then it was all over. The congregation poured out into the sunshine to eat their bread and catch up with whatever gossip they had not managed to fit in during the service.

It was sublime, quite simply sublime. I came out elated, the way you are supposed to feel leaving church, rather than relieved, as if you've just been let out on parole.

I stayed in the camping ground near Plataria for several weeks, while my ribs slowly healed, and I ate a lot of beans, and grew accustomed to the sounds and colours of Greece, and to being in Greece. And then the tranquility of my isolated pitch on the water's edge was shattered by the arrival of some neighbours, and it was time to start thinking about hitting the road again.

Campsites, I'd found, were like tiny leagues of nations, with each nation represented there practicing a different style of camping. Thus campers from the Netherlands liked to travel in groups and formed small friendly Dutch republics wherever they went.

The Greeks also travelled in groups, but much larger groups. They'd take over whole campgrounds, which they would effortlessly turn into small city states. They didn't seem to bother much with travelling to other countries — why would they? They had the whole of Greece on their doorstep, after all.

British campers tended to be retired couples, travelling singly, rather than in groups. Many of those I encountered had given up their permanent homes in the United Kingdom, returning only rarely for visits, and parking in the driveways of grown up children or relatives.

Because their campervans had become their permanent homes, these vehicles tended to be extremely well-kitted out, in often ingenious ways, and as often as not there'd be a dog lying on a rug at their feet, while they sipped their G&Ts under the awning at sundown, or before sundown, or any time after sunrise, in fact. I'm generalizing here, but British campers did seem capable of drinking all the other nations under the camp table singlehanded.

And then there were the Germans. In their natural setting of Germany, Germans doubtless possessed many admirable qualities: efficiency, planning, organizational capability etc., but in a campsite in Greece, these self-same qualities were less straightforwardly virtues.

German campers had the German Campers Bible, I was told, in which were listed all the campsites that were deemed acceptable, and all that were not. It was a good gauge of a campsite's facilities and cleanliness, in fact, whether or not there were Germans there, and unfortunately Plataria Bay was one of those that had made it into the German Campers Bible.

At first glance the new arrivals pulling up in their van alongside my tent didn't seem too alarming. The man, Klaus, hopped out and said "My van will block your way, no?" It seemed unlikely that something so compact and innocuous could block what was, after all, a fairly large piece of ground.

So I stupidly said: "Not at all, there's plenty of room for us both."

It was only when Klaus and his Frau began to unpack that the reality of having German camping neighbours dawned. Was it possible that one compact van could hold so many expanding contents, or that these contents could fill one and a half campsites to overflowing—theirs, and half of mine?

First came two large German motorcycles with associated gear, knee guards and boots and helmets. The motorcycles were followed by two mountain bicycles.

Fair enough—three different forms of road transport were probably not excessive. One had to adapt to the conditions. Then came a generously proportioned folding table with accompanying chairs. There were sun loungers, too, lest the dining chairs prove uncomfortable.

The expanding awning, which expanded greatly, took some time to erect and attach to the van. I now realized that the entrance to Klaus and his Frau's sleeping quarters would be just a couple of feet from the entrance to my tent.

The travelling kitchen was next—a large brazier, about the size of a small refrigerator, provided the means for Herr and Frau Klaus to cook large quantities of German food of an evening in Greece. There was a sack of coal to keep some food hot, and a portable fridge to keep other food cold.

A camping trip to Greece would not be complete without many crates of German beer, and these were stacked next to the fridge, the brazier and the sack of coal. The necessities of life taken care of, including torches as large as car batteries, coils of rope, and portable lanterns, it was time to unload aids to entertainment.

His and her matching surfboards with large sails attached were propped against a tree in front of my tent, partially obscuring my view of Plataria Bay. For calm days, the windsurfing gear was supplemented with an inflatable motorized sailing vehicle. A motor boat? An inflatable mechanized raft? Whatever it was called, it emerged from the van as something quite small and innocuous, but like everything else, it inflated to the size of a small battleship.

When the expanding ladder was produced, the only reason I didn't laugh was because laughing with broken ribs was extremely painful. The ladder allowed access to the expanding contraption on the roof of the van, which billowed up into something the size of a small tent.

Klaus would disappear up into it every now and then. It was a study perhaps, or maybe even a sauna, but whatever its function, it was very effective at blocking out the gentle rays of the evening sun setting over Plataria Bay.

Chapter 10: Shameless Naked People

And so it was that Germans forced the evacuation of yet another foreign beach. But it is as well they did, for leaving the safety and tranquility of Plataria Bay was never going to be easy because I was quite plainly terrified, and this for several reasons.

I'd been in Greece long enough to notice it was nothing like Holland. There was no such thing as a flat road in Greece, and aside from careering up and down in giddy ascents and terrifying descents, the roads were also uneven in quality: occasionally good, occasionally passable, but for the most part potholed, narrow and dangerous, with lots of places I could plummet effortlessly to an instant death.

But the main reason I wanted to hide in Plataria forever was my fear of the dogs of Greece. In this respect Greece was again nothing like Holland. In Holland the dogs had been nicely contained behind neat picket fences, but in Greece dogs pretty much did what they pleased. In remote areas such as this one, what they pleased was forming packs and ripping cyclists to shreds. I am not making this up. I read about it before I left. People had actually died.

To make matters worse, I met an Italian couple who attested in person to the reality of the danger. They had spent a night in the campsite at Plataria where I met them and we got chatting. They were planning to cycle right round Greece and take their time about it and they were full of excitement as they told me all about it. He was going to take photographs, and these he hoped to sell over the internet.

I raised the question of dogs, because it was something of an obsession with me, but the man wasn't in the slightest bit afraid. "I laugh at dogs," he said.

There were times, and this was one of them, when I too would have dearly loved an andras with me to laugh at the dogs of Greece.

Two days later the woman was back, alone and hysterical. Now this was a hardy, athletic type, the sort of woman who wore lycra, and not at all the sort I would have thought prone to nervous hysteria. She was nothing at all like me, in other words, for I *was* prone to nervous hysteria and never once wore lycra.

"I am going back to Italy," she announced, when I asked her what had happened. "He can go on alone, but I am not going any further. I have had enough."

"But why?" I asked.

"The dogs," she said. "We were attacked three times in two days." Her boyfriend had managed to drive them off with the power of his laughter, but she had been so traumatized she was abandoning both her dream and her andras. Next morning she was gone, cycling back to Igoumenitsa to catch the first available ferry back to Italy.

Oh great, I thought, that's just great. And she'd had an andras to drive them off. I would be completely alone.

Aside from the very specific fears of dogs, dangerous roads and lunatic Greek drivers in articulated lorries on mountain passes, there were also many nameless fears, and not least that vague and generalized terror that came from facing an unknown future with goodness knows what horrors contained within it.

But after two days of Herr Klaus and his Frau I'd had enough. They had the same effect on me that Henry had had all those weeks ago in the Netherlands. They forced me to overcome the inertia wrought by fear and get moving again.

So I set off from Plataria shortly after dawn one morning in late May, heading south and taking the main road in the direction of a town called Prevesa.

The decision to follow the main road was the result of weighing up competing evils: the traffic might be thunderous and frightening on the main road, but there was far less chance of an encounter with the canines of Greece. Those I would be more likely to meet on the beautiful but isolated minor roads through the mountains, such as those the Italian couple had taken.

Sometimes all it took was just the initial push to get going again, for after I'd done so, my spirits lifted just as they had done in Holland, and the knot of fear gradually unraveled. It was good to be on the move again. No it was *great* to be on the move again.

It's a feeling I've not had before or since, but one I would love to revisit. There was something so liberating and exhilarating about setting off into a blank canvas of a future, unburdened by possessions and commitments, with no idea where I'd spend the night, let alone the night after that, and my health and welfare entirely in the lap of the gods, or in this case the lap of God.

The land through which I passed was exceedingly beautiful, and in spite of being an arterial route there was not a great deal of traffic after all, and the dogs of my nightmares were conspicuous by their absence.

In a village called Margariti I stopped for a cup of coffee at a small, ramshackle kafenion at the side of the road, with the usual complement of ancients sitting around drinking with the owner, all three talking at once. They were interchangeable these ancients, I saw them everywhere. Courteous, curious and kind, they spent their days sitting outside kafenia, all talking at once in loud voices.

"I am Margaret also," I told the café owner, after assuring everyone that no, I was not German, and that I didn't have an andras. The owner went at once to the flower boxes lining his veranda, plucked a carnation, and presented it to me along with my coffee. "Then it is a very special coffee," he said. And so it was.

It was awkward transporting a wilting flower on a bicycle for 30km in the late morning heat, but seeing it there, fastened to my handlebar bag, filled my heart with joy. I pressed it and dried it that evening, and I have it still.

On my right I passed the Lake of Morph (or Sleep), a surreal, sunken expanse of water filled with vegetation that made it look less like a lake and more like wetlands. The abundant birdlife that flourished there was wheeling and swooping in search of food. It was a rich, lush terrain, and, since the road was relatively flat, it made for pleasant cycling. But that was not to last of course, for it never did.

After Morph I took a 20 km detour through hill country, heading for the nearest camping site, which happened to be near the coastal town of Parga. Parga had been popular with package tourists for many years, something that had rendered it profoundly unattractive. It was all dressed up in clichés, and in spite of being on the mainland, it looked like a caricature of a Greek Island.

The only reason I went there at all was because there were no other campsites within easy reach, but it was a decision I regretted as soon as I got there. The local population wore that jaded and cynical look that I was beginning to recognize wherever tourists were overly-plentiful, and which boded ill for the campsite a little further down the coast, my destination for the night.

I was to discover, as I journeyed south through Greece, that the villages and campgrounds of Greece divided neatly into two extremes. They were either heavenly, or they were hellish. There was almost nothing that fell into the comfortable, purgatorial middle ground. The people were like that too: they were either friendly and obliging to a fault (the majority), or they were obnoxiously rude and unhelpful. Greece I found to be a dichotomous land.

In line with this observation, whenever I wheeled my bicycle into a camping ground, I would either be overwhelmed with the desire to leave at once, or the desire to stay forever. Occasionally I would arrive in a place with the intention of staying just a night or two and then I'd wake up one morning and realize a whole week had slipped by. The man in the little minimarket would reach for a packet of Camels and the lady in the internet cafe would move to turn on Machine Number Three and that's when I'd know it was time to move on.

At the other extreme, there were places where I'd wheel in and wheel straight out again. But escape wasn't always possible, especially if the next campground was twenty kilometers distant and the sun already sinking. The campsite in Parga was one of that sort. It had me trapped, at least for the night. To reach it, I'd had to wheel my bicycle down a road so steep it was impossible to ride it, with palms sweating from the exertion of applying the brakes all the way down, to stop it running away from me. I'd need a night's rest before I'd be capable of tackling that hill, for going up would be a hundred times worse.

When I reached the campsite, which the owners had presumptuously named Paradise, it was immediately apparent that heaven it wasn't. I waited in the empty reception area for someone to serve me, and idly plucked a guide to Greek campsites from the rack of maps and guides on sale there. I opened it to check the level of detail before purchasing it, but I had done no more than glance at it, when the woman who ran the place emerged from some inner sanctum, stormed over, snatched it out of my hands, snapped it shut, and placed it back on the shelf. Then she glared at me. *Charming*, I thought, *just charming*.

If it hadn't been for that awful hill, the fact that the day was advanced, and that it was God knew how many kilometers to the next campsite, but I didn't even know where that might be, because Madam had snatched the guide away, I'd have left at once.

There was nothing for it but to endure a night in paradise and escape at dawn. I pitched tent beneath hundred year olive trees and then, because the day still had a couple of hours to run, followed a short bush path to the beach, which turned out to be a beautiful sandy cove.

Out on the water dozens of specially designed tourist boats were chugging noisily round the bay, each equipped with loud speakers and loud hailers, and all booming out advertisements and bazouki music, discordantly and simultaneously. It was unpleasant, but not as unpleasant as the next thing I noticed.

I settled myself on the sand with my notebook and pen, and turned to glance at the couple lying on the beach to my left, as you do. It took a full five seconds for my brain to interpret the information that was being passed there along the optic nerve.

The man was stark naked and so was his wife. I turned my head hurriedly to the other side, only to find myself staring at another couple, also buck naked. So I fixed my gaze straight ahead, but there was no escaping the spectacle of naked flesh. I'd not noticed them before, but now I saw there were groups of large pink tourists cavorting naked in the waves.

I gathered my belongings hastily and retreated to my tent and thought about how far off the morning seemed. The experience did make me more inclined to forgive the rudeness of the woman in reception, however. *This* must be her overriding perception of northern Europeans—a bunch of shameless naked people.

Greeks, especially those of middle age and older, were usually very modest in their dress. And if I, of more liberal background, had found the naked spectacle offensive, how much more would pious Greek women find it so, those who wore their skirts right down to their ankles.

The incident reminded me of the last time I'd been in Greece, some two decades earlier, and a visit I'd made to the Sporadean island of Patmos, the place where St John received his visions and where he wrote the apocryphal book of Revelations. There I had seen little wooden signs on the beaches bearing the words: *This is a Holly Island. No naked sunbathing*. I had smiled at the time, but now, having had a much clearer look at expanses of naked flesh than I'd ever wanted, I thought Holly Island and its prohibitions against nude sunbathing not nearly so quaintly old-fashioned.

The road from Parga to the larger town of Prevesa at the south-westernmost point of the northern mainland is now just a hazy blur in my memory. The hills had a lot to do with that. Cycling became one long, mind-numbing push of the bike up a seemingly interminable hill, followed by an all too brief glide down the other side, and then up again and down again, over and over. It took several days of this to get to Prevesa.

On the way I spent a night in an unlisted campsite near a village called Lygia. The place was empty, not only of Germans, but of all nationalities, and for reasons that were immediately apparent. It was run down, grubby and poorly equipped. But it had a certain tranquility about it; the adjacent beach was beautiful, and the owners were kindly.

And in a nearby village, well off the beaten track, where goats, sheep and chickens ran freely through the streets, I saw what was surely the most beautiful church in Greece. It was unlocked, so I went inside and the interior took my breath away.

It was a symphony of light and colour and gold and space, impossible to describe, impossible to photograph. I could only stare in wonder. As a proof of the existence of heaven, it was right up there with the ontological, a church of which no finer could be conceived, unless it is heaven itself.

The ride from Lygia to Prevesa was hilly and difficult at first, and, on reaching the next campsite on the route, I found it was closed. There was no choice but to press on. The road flattened on the approaches to Prevesa, which was a mercy, but the day was searingly hot and the traffic had thickened considerably. Trucks now thundered past, dangerously close, causing the bicycle to wobble precariously in their slipstream. The countryside grew ugly and industrialized and Prevesa itself I disliked from the start.

The nearest campsite in a generally southerly direction was on the island of Lefkada some 30km away. Lefkada was not quite an island — it was more of a peninsula separated by an underground tunnel and then a bridge. To get there from Prevesa there were two options. I could go through the tunnel, along with the thundering trucks, or I could cycle all the way round the Ambracian Gulf, a detour of hundreds of kilometers and in quite the wrong direction most of the way. And since my internal compass was saying "go south middle-aged woman," going east wasn't an option.

There was, however, something more than a little disconcerting about the prospect of sharing a dark tunnel with thundering trucks. I would probably end up squashed like a fly against the concrete walls. That's when it occurred to me that bicycles may not even be allowed in the tunnel and that I'd best check first.

I made my way through the confusing street system of Prevesa, it being one of those ugly cities that looked as if it has been thrown there, all haphazard streets and mismatched buildings. Everyone I asked said "no bicycles are allowed in the tunnel."

Fine. I was tired anyway. It had been a long day. I would catch a ferry to Lefkada instead. But down at the harbour there was more bad news. There were no ferries from Prevesa to Lefkada.

I was growing desperate. Prevesa was having that now familiar effect large towns had had on me ever since Holland: they made me feel panicky and trapped, and simultaneously lonely and isolated. And this one had me quite literally trapped.

I tried a travel agency. "I have a bicycle," I said. "I want to go to Lefkada, but it appears to be impossible."

The woman behind the desk nodded. "It is impossible. There is no way of travelling to Lefkada by bicycle."

"What about the bus?" I already knew that bicycles were not permitted on buses in Greece, but perhaps they made an exception in the case of Lefkada.

The woman shook her head again. "No. It is not possible to take a bicycle on the bus."

"But what do people with bicycles do if they want to go south?"

She shrugged. She didn't care what people with bicycles trying to escape from Prevesa did.

To all intents and purposes I was stuck in a horrible, noisy Greek town with no prospect of travelling south. The only way to travel south was to travel north, and then a long way east, before eventually south would become possible again.

I did not want to go east, and I most certainly did not want to go north. I'd just come from the north. I had had enough of the north. I wanted to go south. No, I had to go south. There's no arguing with an internal compass.

So I'd try my luck at the bus station, I decided. There must be *some* way for cyclists to travel to Lefkada. I would not be the first who needed to do so, surely.

"Certainly," said the helpful young man in the ticket office. It will not be a problem for you to take your bicycle on the bus."

111

"Thank you," I burst out, in my bad Greek. "I was afraid I would have to stay in Prevesa forever." The small crowd around the ticket office laughed because they understood perfectly — they were also all buying tickets out of the place.

Greece was like that. There were plenty of stupid rules and regulations. It was like Belgium in that way, but there was a life-giving difference. Unlike Belgium, in Greece these rules were never set in concrete. There was a flexibility that could be exercised in the direction of common sense and humanity. And while it was not usual for bicycles to be permitted on buses, here, in this situation, where there was clearly no other way for me to go south, the rules were adjusted accordingly.

When the bus for Lefkada arrived, the driver looked sourly at my bicycle, and I feared the friendly, pragmatic ruling would be overruled. But the helpful young man from the ticket office anticipated just such an eventuality, and emerged to smooth things over with a few words and a joke. He even helped me load the bicycle into the luggage compartment, because this was Greece and not Belgium, France or Italy; it was a land where chivalry was still very much alive. And thus I was transported by bus to the island of Lefkada in a country where bicycles were not allowed on buses.

Lefkada was an unmemorable place on the whole, except for a couple of the people I met there, and were it not for them, I'd probably skip over both Lefkada and Kefalonia, and jump straight to the point where my journey rejoined the Greek mainland on the Peloponnese peninsula. For I didn't linger on either island, I just kept on moving south.

I'd experienced once before this powerful urge to travel in a particular direction of the compass. It was in Auckland, New Zealand, and I'd just moved there with Polly. We were looking for rental accommodation in the north of the city and we'd been looking for days, but found nothing. I knew deep down we were wasting our time, and that we needed to go west.

This wasn't because accommodation was more plentiful in the west. It wasn't based on any objective information, in fact. It was just a curiously powerful tug of the internal compass, a strong intuition with no logical basis. And so we went west. As I pointed the car in the direction of Auckland's western suburbs, both Polly and I experienced a curious lifting of the spirits.

And, after days of fishing and taking nothing in the north, within hours we'd found an apartment in the west that was perfectly suitable, but more importantly, I'd learned to heed and respect that internal guide, which applies to literal points of the compass as well as metaphorical ones.

Chapter 11: Lefkada's Finest

On the Island of Lefkada I met a large and ancient man called Spiros. He had a supermarket in the middle of nowhere, although supermarket is a bit of a misnomer here. Every village in Greece had one or two emporia that were, in effect, no larger than the average corner shop, but known and labeled as 'supermarkets.' In the larger towns there were real supermarkets, of course, but Spiros' supermarket was not one of those. It was tiny and cramped, and bore all the signs of having seen better days. The goods on the shelves were ancient and dusty and there were packets there that were so sun-faded it was no longer possible to make out if they contained washing powder or cereal.

I bought a tin of beans, figuring ten-year-old tinned beans would be safer than any of the other ten-year-old goods on offer and exchanged a few words in Greek. Spiros arose at once from his stool behind the counter and engulfed me in a great bear hug in honour of my efforts to speak his language.

He beckoned me to follow him, and led me through the narrow maze of little shelves to an alcove at the rear of the shop, where he produced a large unlabelled bottle of bootleg brandy. "Lefkas' finest," he said proudly. "Have you ever tasted the finest brandy of Lefkas?"

I had not, so he poured two generous cupfuls and we sat down in his un-peopled supermarket to discuss whatever limited subjects my Greek vocabulary would allow. We were getting on like a house on fire, thanks to Lefkas' finest, but then two smartly dressed men in shiny suits and dark glasses arrived to spoil our party. From Spiros' reaction I gathered this was not good news. To my untrained eye they looked like members of the Mob, but perhaps they were tax-collectors, or maybe the bootleg squad. Whoever they were, Spiros shrank visibly at sight of them and I made good my escape.

Evidently they'd not called by to execute a kneecapping, for the next day when I had cause to cycle past Spiros' shop again, he looked as cheerful as before. He was sitting on a battered stool in the early morning sun, drinking Lefkas' finest brandy. He arose at once and beckoned enthusiastically. "Come and drink some of Lefkas' finest with me…" But it was 8.30 in the morning and 8.30am was too early for brandy, even for me, although clearly not for Spiros.

I remember absolutely nothing about the campsite on Lefkada where I spent two nights, except the Albanian couple who were employed to keep the place clean. The woman cleaned the toilets, the man tended the grounds. This was a common sight in Greece: the influx of Albanian immigrants willing to work for very little meant they were often found doing the less attractive jobs.

But this particular young man did not have enough to occupy his time and appeared to find me and my bicycle fascinating. He spent most of the time I was there sweeping the path right outside my tent and peering at me curiously, and that's why I remember him. It was not a little disconcerting to have a strange man staring at me while I warmed up fasolakia on my little oil primus.

With my original daily budget of €15 pretty much slashed in half by the Financial Crisis, and my funds supplemented only by occasional earnings from proofreading, it is fair to say I did not eat very extravagantly in Greece. A simple tent pitch cost €5, and that left very little for everything else. So I ate a lot of fasolakia (green beans in tomato sauce), which came in tins and which cost just cents. I also ate a lot of some or other type of beans, also in a tomato sauce, whose name I forget. I ate bread, too, lots of it, and my luxury item was honey and yoghurt, because Greek honey and yoghurt were to die for, as anyone who has tasted them will surely confirm.

Whenever possible I drank and I would have drunk a lot more if I could have afforded it. I'm not particularly proud of drinking my way through Greece, but it's what I did whenever I could. A bottle of cheap retsina was my reward for a tough day's cycling; it was something to look forward to, something to get me up those hills, something to ease the loneliness of evenings spent in a tent, listening to Leonard Cohen on the world's oldest mini-CD player.

To return to the Albanian man who stared at me as I ate my fasolakia and drank my retsina, I had by this time realized that the best camping grounds in Greece were the ones that were the most unkempt. Not only were they not in the German Camping Bible, but they did not have the obligatory little man popping up around my tent, busying himself with unnecessary and irritating trimming and sweeping, cutting and watering.

I caused a bit of a stir wherever I went, something I didn't fully understand at the time, but I think it had to do with the fact people were not often seen cycling through Greece, and certainly not a woman without an andras, with nothing but a tent, a primus, and a bedroll. So I was something of an attraction, like an exhibit in a museum, or an act in a circus.

It all became tiresomely predictable. I would arrive in a campsite, choose the most isolated and private pitch possible, and then set up tent. Within minutes out would come the little man with his saw, his hose, or his broom, and he'd busy himself round and about my tent, taking a good long look at my gear, my self, and my bicycle. Sometimes we'd get chatting, sometimes not. There was nothing sinister about it; I never felt threatened by it. It was just plain, old-fashioned curiosity.

Not remotely tempted to linger on Lefkada, I discovered the ferry for the island of Kefalonia departed twice daily from the southern port of Vassiliki. The way there was through mountains and the day was unsettled. High in the hills between my camping ground and Vassiliki, dark clouds were gathering to my right and they were moving closer. They looked to be the sort of clouds capable of bearing vast quantities of water. Rain in Greece was as dramatic as everything else: the heavens literally opened and within seconds there were torrents of water hurtling down roads, drainpipes and gutters. I had experienced one or two of these storms, but only from the relative shelter of my tent.

Here in the hills of Lefkada there was no shelter, not a house in sight and very few trees. I pedaled on in hope of finding something in time, for I could tell from the look of the sky that I had just minutes before the downpour. It was not so much my person I was concerned about, it was the oldest laptop in the world and my camera, both inadequately protected in none-too-watertight pannier bags.

Just as the air turned freezing cold, the prelude to rain, and the sky was split by a dramatic bolt of lightning, I rounded a bend and there, at the side of the road, was a builder's hut. A man was hastening to cover his stacks of timber. He saw me and beckoned and we both ran for the shelter of his hut.

It poured for a solid hour, accompanied by lightning bolts and claps of thunder. We huddled in his hut, while he made us coffee on a primitive wood stove, the best cup of coffee I have ever tasted. We talked — or rather, we struggled to talk, and at one point he picked up an ancient Bible (in Greek), and opened it to the book of Timotheos, announcing that it was after the biblical Timothy that he had been named. The original Timothy would have been proud of him, I thought, proud of the way he'd offered shelter and refreshment so warm-heartedly to a random stranger on a bicycle, as if doing so was the most natural thing in the world.

Finally, the rain stopped, I offered my heartfelt thanks to this further example of Lefkada's finest, and carried on my way to the port of Vassiliki, reflecting that had I been a more conventional traveller, snug in my car or my campervan, I would never have met Timotheos, and enjoyed traditional Greek hospitality of a kind that restored my faith in humanity, in a builder's hut in the mountains, while we sheltered from a dramatic display of elemental fury.

The tiny port of Vassiliki was home for one more night and then it was onwards by ferry to the island of Kefalonia. From its northern tip (where the ferry disembarked) to its southern extremities (where I left for the Peloponnese peninsula a few days later), Kefalonia was stunningly beautiful.

I cycled on a remote mountain road where my only companions were eagles, and where the only human I saw for half a day was an ancient lady, dressed in black, hobbling along, a bundle of twigs on her back, looking for all the world like a figure out of a children's illustrated bible.

The coast road on the east side of Kefalonia boasted some of the finest scenery in Greece. High in the mountains above the sea, I looked down upon tiny villages and half-moon beaches far below, each sheltered on three sides by sheer cliff faces.

I met a young man at one of these cliff top lookout points. We had both stopped to take photographs. My bicycle chose that moment to fall over, something it did often, and he came over at once to help me. This was Greece, after all.

"Don't worry," I said in Greek, "I am fine. It happens all the time."

"Never before have I met a foreigner who has bothered to learn my language," he said. Little did he know how little of his language I knew. Had we conversed much longer I would have been found out.

When he went back to his car he paused, and impulsively returned, holding out a a box of cinnamon sweets. "Here," he said, "here's something sweet for you, something sweet for the road."

I was charmed. Charmed and delighted. This was the real Greece, the real deal. Where else in the world would such a thing happen? Nowhere I had ever been, before or since.

My opinion of Kefalonia was to plummet somewhat before the day was out, because that is the way life seems to work. Sami, the location of my next campsite, was truly dreadful. It was attractive, certainly, the beachfront and surrounding hills were lovely, but everywhere were the signs of a tourist corruption of the worst kind.

And all this because in 2000, Nicolas Cage, a vast film crew, and an army of extras descended on Sami for the filming of Captain Corelli's Mandolin. From the look and feel of the place you would have thought it had happened just yesterday. There was Captain Corelli's Bar, Corelli's café, and dozens of other variations on a mandolin theme.

But the worst thing about it was the license this seemed to give the local community to charge like wounded bulls. Not only had Nicholas Cage made one of the worst films ever here, but he'd also caused financial difficulty ever after for anyone travelling through without a Hollywood-sized pocket book.

It cost some ridiculous amount like €7 an hour to use the internet, pots of honey were twice the price of anywhere else, and in the campsite, they even charged for use of the refrigerator.

The young woman on reception in the campsite sighed at mention of Captain Corelli. The crew had stayed in the campsite site during the filming, she said, and the entire village had been required to dress up in period costume for the duration. I asked her if she had seen it.

"Yes," she said, pulling a face. "Nicholas Cage's worst ever performance…that accent…" And we both laughed unkindly at Nicholas Cage's attempt at an Italian accent which is the only thing I can clearly remember about the entire film, except that it was spectacularly awful.

"It was good for the village, but it was also bad for the village," she said. And I could see why. The village was now making a killing from tourists with their over-inflated prices, but they'd managed in the process to kill off every last vestige of its traditional charm.

After Sami it was onward by ferry again, this time to Killini, where I'd be back on the mainland of Greece, in the top left-hand corner of the Peloponnesian peninsula, which no-one had ruined yet, by making a movie there.

Chapter 12: Almost Utopia

"When a Greek sees a tourist, he sees a ten euro note with legs." So said Kostas, my new friend, and he was allowed to say stuff like that because he was Greek. I was in the village of Kastro, and I thought I'd died and gone to heaven. If ever a place captured the essence of Greece—unspoilt, free of tourists, yet picture perfect and charming—it was Kastro, the antithesis of Kefalonia's Sami in every way.

I'd reached Kastro after cycling seven kilometers through fragrant lemon and olive groves from the tiny port of Killini, where the ferry from Kefalonia had deposited me. Now early June, thousands of baby olives covered the branches, preparing to swell and ripen through the hot sun of a Greek summer, but for their part, the lemons were already heavy and starting to drop.

I rounded a corner and there was Kastro, and it was a stop the bicycle and get out the camera moment, because Kastro wasn't called Kastro for nothing. Chlemoutsi Castle (Kastro) was almost as large as the village itself and dominated the landscape for miles around.

On the westernmost promontory of the Peloponnese peninsula, Kastro was well and truly off the beaten track. The main road south from the port of Patras, where most tourists landed on the Peloponnese, bypassed this area completely and dashed on to Pyrga and Olympia, taking the tourist stream with it.

But Kastro didn't need tourists, Kostas told me. It was olive trees that sustained life in Kastro, lending themselves to a peaceful, simple life. Olive trees contributed also to the great beauty of the region. Wherever the road took me in the area, it led through olive groves, and olive groves were extraordinarily beautiful.

People lived and died by the olives, and from all accounts, they died a lot later than those who did not enjoy their benefits. "My mother is 94," said Kostas, "And her good health is all down to the oil." He had a small shop in Kastro, and plenty to say for himself and he said it in English, which was always a bonus.

"You know what we Greeks did when the Euro came?" he said. "Did we bother to get out our calculators and do maths? No, of course we didn't. We just moved the decimal point."

"The day before the Euro came," he said, "souvlaki cost 150 drachma. Next day, souvlaki was on sale everywhere for €1.50." (Souvlaki is a traditional Greek snack of small pieces of meat cooked on a skewer.)

"That was an increase of about 200 percent. Now if you apply this principle across the board, in a land where wages remained the same because employers *did* get out their calculators and do the maths, it's easy to see why ordinary Greeks have struggled so much since the introduction of the euro."

If money was going out, people took the trouble to calculate it properly, but if money was coming in, they simply moved the decimal point. "Some people got very rich, but most people got a lot poorer," he said.

While once it had been possible to enjoy a simple, but comfortable life on the minimum wage, or from a modest income such as a pension, now it was not. This explained why, everywhere I went, I heard people, especially the elderly, grumbling about the euro.

Kostas was one of the nicest people I met in Greece, but it was in Kastro that I also met one of the worst. I spent my first night in a place called Camping Sophia, which was run by the eponymous Sophia, a woman of advanced age with some sort of cast in her eye, who both looked and behaved like a witch, and I do not use that term lightly.

I took a dislike to Camping Sophia the moment I got there, but Sophia was one step ahead of me. She snatched my passport from me the second I arrived, and was so intimidating in demeanor in spite of her diminutive size; I did not have the courage to ask for it back. (Some but not all campsite owners demanded the handover of passports to ensure that payment was effected before departure.)

I'd realized too late there was another campsite a few kilometers down the coast called Camp Fournia, which would surely be better than Camping Sophia. It could hardly be any worse. But with my passport held hostage, I was stuck there for at least one night.

I pitched tent reluctantly to the grating sound of Sophia in the reception area, some distance away, shouting at her employees at the top of her voice. The shouting went on throughout the afternoon and well into the evening. For such a tiny old lady, she had a fine pair of lungs.

It was not pleasant, camping to the accompaniment of shouting. I had grown accustomed to camping to the sound of cicadas, doves, sparrows and frogs. Shouting was an unwelcome addition to the symphony. The place was packed with miserable people just like me, packed cheek by jowl into too-small pitches, all listening to the shouting, and all also wishing they were somewhere else.

I fell asleep at last, but not for long. Sometime in the middle of the night I was woken by more terrible shouting. It took a few minutes to understand what was going on, because it was hard to believe the evidence of my ears, but Sophia was going from tent to tent waking people up.

I stuck my head out the tent flap to have a look. There was pandemonium. Furious campers were emerging from their tents, caravans and campervans and joining in the shouting. There was shouting in many languages now, just like Babel.

Apparently someone had parked their car in the wrong place, and Sophia wasn't willing to let the matter rest till morning. She decided to wake everyone up, find out who the culprit was, and make them move it.

In the morning it was pouring with rain, and the prospects of escape from Camping Sophia did not look promising. There was the oldest laptop in the world to consider and I was careful always not to travel in the rain for fear of damaging it. But such was my aversion to Camping Sophia, I packed up anyway, and went to sit under cover on the balcony of the taverna, and to wait for the rain to ease.

There had been since dawn a steady exodus of cars and campervans. No-one wanted to spend another night in Camping Sophia. I envied them their watertight means of escape, and as the rain continued to pour, my desperation increased. At last it eased and I seized the moment to reclaim my passport.

The old hag was reluctant to let me go. "You are going? So soon? Why you no stay longer?"

Because you are a horrible old harridan. In a remarkable display of self-unawareness, she failed to make the connection between her own behaviour and her desperately fleeing campers and seemed genuinely surprised by it.

I've since looked up Camping Sophia on the internet. (Not its real name, mind you.) Some years have elapsed, and the nine reviews there all seem very positive, although some are in German, so I can't be entirely sure. Perhaps Sophia has now retired. Sometimes it's just hard to believe people are writing about the same place.

I have also looked up the campsite I escaped to, a place called Camp Fournia, which was heaven on earth. I wanted to stay there forever. But there's a review on the website that complains about it at length, also describing a place I don't recognize. I am also aware that some reading this book, who have been to some of the places I have recorded, may also struggle to recognize them. Italy for example, and Belgium.

But whatever the philosophical questions about perception and truth underpinning all that, I ended up staying many days in Camp Fournia, even though I'd not intended to, and doing so gave me the opportunity to get to know the area well, and that included the castle.

Here, as in so many other stunning historical sites, I had the place to myself.

There was an outer enclosure and an inner courtyard, both ringed with tunnelled walls wide enough to drive a bus through. I sat in the warm early morning sunshine in the outer enclosure and listened to a silence broken only by the wings of ravens and the occasional sound of a mallet striking stone from one of the two masons at work on an ongoing restoration project.

It was hard to believe this peaceful place had been the scene of frequent massacres and bloodshed. But it had, and there were even the remains of a machicolation to prove it. A machicolation was a charming hot oil and rock hurtling device that did what it said on the tin: it rained hot oil and rocks down on anyone attempting to storm the castle. It was probably one of Sophia's ancestors who'd been in charge of firing it, in fact.

In the camp near Kastro, I had the most idyllic of campsites. I was sole occupant of a tiny headland and I looked out each morning across the Ionian Sea towards the islands of Kefalonia and Zakinthos. I didn't even mind the inevitable tiresome digging/weeding/cutting man who showed up to hang round my tent on the pretext of doing something useful.

For Dimitri was a digging/weeding/cutting man with a difference: he was also a philosopher and a poet, and he quoted Plato and Homer and Cavafy in between shovelling spadefuls of dirt. He didn't speak much English, but between his basic English and my basic Greek we understood each other well enough. He pointed to an island in the distance. "That is Ithaca," he said. "There Homer travelled and there our great poet Cavafy pilgrimed in his imagination."

I took a photograph of Dimitri, caught unawares in his working clothes. The next few times I saw him he was all dolled up in a suit and tie, digging the earth like a fashion model. He couldn't understand why I didn't want to photograph him dressed like that, but now I so wish I had done so, for it would have made for a much more interesting photograph.

My new life in Greece delivered up many sublime moments, but it also had plenty of dark moments. The Financial Crisis that had begun in Nice was now unfolding in earnest, with the battle to free my frozen travel funds waged in the internet café in Kastro. Here I discovered something I had long suspected: that banking officials are as uncooperative as they are stupid. I discovered also how helpless I was to elicit their assistance from a distance of thousands of kilometers, with just an overpriced email facility ticking away at a rate of three Euros an hour as a means of communication.

"No!" typed the Neteller support person. "You may not make a wire transfer because you are not currently in your country of residence. You may order a cheque. Thank you for banking with Neteller."

The reasoning made no sense. There probably was none. But it seemed there was no other way forward, and even though I had one of those sinking premonitions it was all going to go horribly wrong, I went ahead and ordered one anyway, and had it sent to Polly, who said she would bank it on my behalf.

Polly, aged 80, expended considerable effort hobbling off to the nearest branch of Kiwibank armed with the newly arrived cheque and a deposit slip. She was not anticipating any problems depositing it into my account. What possible problems could there be? It wasn't as if she was trying to *withdraw* money from my account.

The news was not good. *The manager told me I am not allowed to deposit a foreign cheque into someone else's account,* she wrote in an email.

And thus began an interminable correspondence with someone called Jayne who worked in Complaints at Kiwibank.

"Yes, certainly," wrote Jayne, "It's not a problem. Of course your mother can deposit the cheque on your behalf, just so long as it is signed on the back by yourself. Thank you for banking with Kiwibank."

"If I was in a position to sign the reverse of the cheque," I wrote back, "I would not need my mother to bank it for me. I would be able to bank it myself."

"Yes, that's fine," she replied, "Certainly your mother may bank it, provided it is endorsed on the back....Thank you for banking with Kiwibank."

Eventually, some couple of dozen emails later, Kiwibank finally agreed to let Polly bank the cheque on my behalf.

"It will take 25 working days to clear," wrote Jayne.

It took three months. In the meanwhile I was continuing my correspondence with Neteller to try and sort something out about the balance of my funds. They finally agreed to let me have a wire transfer and joyfully I ordered one.

"We need the correct SWIFT code of Kiwibank," they told me. A SWIFT code is, I believe, a sort of shorthand identification that facilitates the speedy movement of funds transfers about the globe, ensuring they don't end up in the wrong bank, and the wrong account. So it was back to Jayne at Kiwibank with sinking heart, for I had lost confidence in Jayne at Kiwibank.

"Kiwibank does not have a SWIFT code," wrote Jayne. "The wire transfer will need to be made through an intermediary bank. Thank you for banking with Kiwibank."

I got on the Neteller live chat thing and repeated the message from Jayne, providing the SWIFT code of one of the intermediary banks that she had mentioned.

"No," typed Neteller support. "Kiwibank *does* have a SWIFT code, and we have already transferred your funds, using this code. Is there anything else we can help you with today? Thank you for banking with Neteller."

In a cold sweat of panic I emailed Kiwibank with the news. After a delay of a week or two (she was on holiday, I think, relaxing somewhere without a care in the world), Jayne emailed back.

"Yes," wrote Jayne, "Kiwibank does indeed have a SWIFT code, but we don't tell customers that, because it only works on local transactions. Your wire transfer will not find its way into your account using that code. Thank you for banking with Kiwibank."

So now I had a wire transfer located somewhere in International Banking Cyberspace, having slipped into a big black hole of incompetence, and a cheque that was going to take months to clear. And so it went on — day after day of frustrating correspondence and the seemingly impossible task of accessing the bulk of my travel funds.

Leaving Kastro was difficult, even more difficult than leaving Plataria had been. I liked the people, and the surrounding countryside was my kind of country. The vegetation was the right shade of green; the sea was the right shade of blue. I considered trying to build a life there, renting an apartment, settling down, emailing Polly and saying, "This is it. I've found Utopia." But for some reason I couldn't do it, because there was something missing.

I had not yet *arrived*, and I knew it. It was almost Utopia, but not quite. There was some deep impulse still pulling me in a southerly direction. The internal compass was saying I'd not gone far enough south.

For all that, I did make a rare and voluntary detour to the east, because to pass within 40 km of the ancient city of Olympia and not visit there would have been an act of the crassest philistinism. Apart from being for centuries the most important spiritual, cultural, and sporting centre in the ancient world, Olympia was also the site of one of the original Seven Wonders of the World. Here had stood a 21 meter statue of Zeus, father of the Greek Gods. That's the equivalent of a four storey building, which is quite staggeringly tall, given how primitive would have been the tools used to fashion it. It's not there anymore, having been destroyed at some uncertain point in history, but the place where it stood is still there, and, with a little imagination, it is possible to envisage it yet.

Ancient Olympia was glorious, but the new Olympia, the tourist-tat town that had grown up around it to cater for the vast numbers who called by there, was not. I stayed two nights, in a terrible camping ground along with dozens of underfed cats and it rained a great deal, which is always a miserable business in a tent, as people who camp in Britain know full well.

I visited ancient Olympia early in the morning, before the tour buses built up to convoy proportions. A lightning bolt and a thunderclap welcomed me, and then the doors of the heavens opened, emptying the sky in a torrential downpour. There was scarcely any shelter among the ruins and so I ran to the entrance of the stadium, where there was a stone arch, and through which others had run before me, only a lot more proficiently, and waited for the storm to pass.

As I stood beneath my stone umbrella, it was almost possible to hear, mingled with the sound of rain on stone, the pounding feet of the ghostly athletes on their way into the stadium. Sodden with rain, the stadium was now just a deserted muddy track, surrounded by grassy banks, but once up to 50,000 spectators had sat there, watching the original Olympians deliver performances worthy of Zeus.

Olympia was place of ghosts, of shades: I could feel them everywhere, and there were some fairly impressive ones among them. Emperor Nero had had a temporary residence there in the first century AD, and that was one man you wouldn't want to cross, dead or alive. There was a more agreeable shade on the far side of the complex, where in a now ruined workshop, the sculptor Phidias had crafted the giant statue of Zeus from gold and ivory. I sat on an ancient stone seat, maybe it was *his* ancient stone seat, and imagined him hammering and chiseling away.

It was still early in the morning, but already the tour buses were coming and going every half hour. Their occupants had just enough time to whizz quickly round before crossing Olympia off that list of places that must be seen in Greece. And in a curious and unintentional parody of the opening ceremonies of modern day Olympic Games, the tour guides held placards bearing numbers or names, such as "Group 12" or "Olympic Tours," as they marched their charges round the ancient city in teams. They also carried whistles to round up any strays in a carefully timed race to fit in another ancient site or two before dinner-time.

I left Olympia and headed back towards the coast. The compass within was happy and the country roads were charming. All was well with the world, Zeus was in his heaven, and I was happy and free as a bird. And then I saw the dogs.

By now dog-fear had reached phobic proportions. I'd seen a lot of them, and what I'd seen, I hadn't liked. Greek people tend not to think of their dogs as pets. They don't take them for walks on leads, or to doggie parlours for a shampoo and cut; they don't dress them in waistcoats in winter, and they don't let them sleep on their beds. Half the Greek canines are functional beasts, used for guarding or herding things. The other half are wild, and have turned feral.

Either way, every time I saw a dog, I developed chronic shortness of breath and heart palpitations. But I also learned that dogs were as varied as humans, and that there were good ones and bad ones, that there were also some with a sense of humour and to that point I'd survived them.

The feral dogs were the ones I'd originally feared the most, but they turned out to be more afraid of me than I was of them, and generally bolted in terror at the first sight of my bicycle. Then there were the dogs that were just having a laugh. These would lurk behind fences or gates until I was right alongside, when they'd jump up and let loose a volley of barking, causing me to swerve in fright, which they seemed to enjoy very much.

It was the second category, the shepherds and farmers' dogs, from which I had the most to fear. Mostly they were chained up and had to make do with snarling, but even chained dogs made me nervous. What if the chains were to snap? What if the next dog I encountered was not chained? The farming dogs of Greece were ferociously territorial and trained to guard their patch against all comers.

And now, up ahead of me, on a lonely country road between Olympia and goodness knows where, two dogs the size of small wolves, definitely belonging to Category Two, were stood in the middle of the road, waiting for me.

They weren't barking, and their tails weren't wagging. They looked mean and purposeful, and when they started to move towards me I broke into an icy terrified sweat.

There's conflicting advice about what to do in situations such as these, and this was something I'd researched with a kind of horrified fascination before I began my trip. Some experts suggested you got off the bicycle and spoke nicely to them. This was meant to disarm them or something, but I had no confidence whatsoever in this approach.

Others said you should just keep pedaling and pretend you hadn't noticed them. I did not think that was such a crash hot idea either.

A third suggestion was to wave a stick and shout loudly. I liked the sound of that one, but there was no stick handy, and besides there were two of them and just one of me. What if they did that wolfish maneuver where one attacks you from the front, and the other one slips round the back? I'd read about that too.

It was a dreadful moment. The farmhouse behind them appeared deserted. There was no one in sight I could call out to. Turning and fleeing would presumably excite the prey drive, and I did not kid myself I could outcycle them. So I got off my bike, put it in front of me as a kind of shield — not that it would have been any use against two of them — stood stock still, and sent up a desperate prayer for help. If ever I needed a miracle it was then, because they were advancing towards me in that half-crouching position. I was no expert in the body language of dogs, but it didn't take an expert to see there was nothing good about the half-crouching position.

I'd not seen a car for hours. It was a lonely country road, a back road, one that I'd taken to avoid the traffic pouring in and out of Olympia. Then out of absolutely nowhere, as if my prayer had summoned it, and I do believe it had, a vehicle appeared behind me.

The driver saw the dogs, noted my precarious situation, and with timing that couldn't have been more perfect, maneuvered the car between me and the dogs, cutting them off and mercifully distracting them. They went crazy, snapping at his tyres, and snarling in a manner that was truly bloodcurdling. I have no doubt that is what they intended to do to me. I was an interloper on their territory and they were protecting their patch. It could have all gone very badly indeed.

The man waved me on, "Quick!" he shouted. "Go!" I didn't need telling. I pedaled like a mad woman until I'd gained the safety of distance, where, looking back, I saw he was still distracting them. When he was confident I was far enough away, he pulled off, overtaking me with a smile and a cheerful wave.

It was a moment of quite extraordinary grace, of providence. There's a naturalistic explanation as well: coincidence. But I don't really believe in coincidence.

Chapter 13: Utopia at Last

In many countries and New Zealand is one, the women often complain there aren't enough decent, available men to go around. The good ones are already taken and the bad ones — well, nobody wants one of those.

The men of rural Greece had the opposite problem. There was an epidemic shortage of single women in the small towns and villages. Women tended to flee to the cities at a young age, uninterested in the prospect of marriage to a farmer and all that went with it. The men would have left too, but someone had to stay behind to care for the land, and that someone was inevitably the son of the family.

This was certainly the case in Zacharo, a small rural town in the province of Ilea, my next port of call after the run in with the dogs. I stayed in a campsite near this ugly-beautiful town for the best part of a week.

Zacharo literally means sugar, but Sugar Town would have won no beauty contests. It was not hard to see why there were problems attracting the right kind of gal: it was outwardly charmless, and even the town church was a bit of a dump, a rare thing indeed.

The population of Zacharo was about 5,000, but the ratio of men to women was an uncomfortable 60:40, with most of the female population elderly. They could be seen, dressed in black, perambulating slowly round the town with the aid of walking sticks.

Then, in a story of optimism triumphing over experience, temporarily at least, the mayor won re-election by promising the men of Sugar Town that they would have brides. For he had heard that in Russia the women had the opposite problem: a chronic shortage of marriageable men.

A trip was planned; a coach-load of country bumpkin bachelors set off from Zacharo across Europe in pursuit of Russian brides. The Russian city of Kiln, eight kilometers from Moscow, was where the romantic exchange was to take place.

A film producer called Kimon Tsakiris recorded this extraordinarily idealistic expedition to woo ladies from afar. Titled *Sugar Town – the Bridegrooms,* it shows, among other things, the men of Zacharo learning how to say *I Love You* in Russian, and jogging along the beach in an attempt to lose excess weight and thereby render themselves more attractive to the ladies of Russia.

Alas, the ladies of Russia turned out to be a disappointment. They were hard-bitten and tough, and the naïve bachelors of Zacharo were no match for them, so there were no fairytale endings. There's an online review that sums up the optimistic experiment: "Despite the mayor's promises, organized luncheons, dark nightclub outings and TV hype, love is harder than anyone assumes. Marital bliss turns out to be more elusive than the Greek bridegrooms thought it would." (Angelike Contis)

I left Zacharo reluctantly to continue my journey south, heading in the direction of a village called Methoni, and this for the simple reason it was the furthest south I could go without having to swim somewhere. En route I stopped briefly in the nearby village of Pilos, and there I managed to disgrace myself at the recently renovated Byzantine castle.

I asked the surly ticket seller where the toilets were, and she replied that they were closed till 3pm. Or at least that's what I thought she said. I thought it sounded a bit odd at the time, but perhaps they were closed for cleaning. Then, in the delight of exploring the romantically deserted castle, I forgot all about it.

What she'd actually said was that the castle itself closed at 3pm, and that 3pm was when she stopped being a surly ticket seller and went off and did stuff she enjoyed. Oblivious to the deadline, I ambled at a leisurely pace round the place, smelt the daisies, climbed the towers, relaxed on benches to take in the view, and 3pm came and went. All the while the surly ticket seller was growing ever surlier, trapped in her stifling ticket box.

It was gone 4pm when I made my way back to the entrance. She was by this time pacing up and down in a fury. She had locked the gates, and what she had actually said dawned on me in one of those moments no amount of apology or groveling is ever going to fix, so there was nothing for it but to collect my bicycle and scuttle shame-facedly away as fast as I could.

The road out of Pilos, heading towards Methoni, began with a fierce hill. The late afternoon sun was blazingly hot, for the Greek summer day was at its hottest between 2pm and 6pm. But then I crested its highest point and saw with relief that from there the road eased gently downhill all the way to Methoni, which I could just make out in the distance as a cluster of tiny orange and white matchboxes and a glint of blue sea.

All too often a fierce uphill was followed by an even fiercer downhill, with the respite from pushing all too brief, so this gentle descent through olive groves was pure pleasure. There was no feeling quite like the one that came from freewheeling down a gentle slope, wind in my hair, and not a care in the world. (I had plenty of cares, but in moments like those it was easy to forget them.)

Just before Methoni, the main road veered off in the direction of Finikounda, Koroni, and ultimately Kalamata and the Mani peninsula. The main stream of traffic, not that it was particularly heavy in these parts since most of it had been siphoned off further north, bypassed Methoni altogether. It was getting late, and I was tired, so I thought I'd spend one night in Methoni, and then head on for Kalamata, where perhaps I'd take the ferry to Crete. I might even travel onwards to Athens. It really didn't matter, for I had no set plans.But now, quite unexpectedly, the drive to keep moving south disappeared and was replaced with an equally strong desire to find somewhere to settle, preferably somewhere in the vicinity of Methoni.

This may have had to do with the fact that I'd reached the southernmost point of the westernmost finger of the Peloponnese peninsular and going south was no longer an option. Or it may have had to do with the fact that I'd been on the road for months now, and life without a bed, a bath, and an internet connection was starting to wear a little thin.

Besides there was Polly to consider. Polly had taken that casual invitation to do something irrevocable and foolish very seriously. She'd boxed up all the books she couldn't bear to part with, and they were all ready to post off to Greece. All she needed was an address to post them to. She'd sorted out medical issues, pension issues, and she'd ordered a new passport. As soon as I issued the green light, she'd be on her way to join me, and so would I please hurry up, she said, and issue the green light. And since Polly is the leading lady in the closing chapters of this adventure, here might be a suitable place to introduce her more fully.

Polly was born in 1929 in Liverpool, of predominantly Welsh ancestry. An only child of a quite formidable mother (I still remember the temper tantrums of my elderly grandmother, they were truly spectacular), she'd been just fourteen when World War II broke out.

War disrupted everything, not least because Liverpool was a major target for German bombing raids, and so between the ages of fourteen and nineteen, Polly experienced air raid shelters, rationing, and the general overthrowal of any kind of life that could be described as normal.

In later life she tended to romanticize this period, and looked back upon these as the best days of her life, as well as the best days of Britain's collective life. It was Britain's finest hour, as far as she was concerned, and perhaps it was. She would devour soppy World War II romance novels by the dozen. If a book had a picture of a Wren or a WRAC on the cover, with bombed out buildings in the background, she just had to read it.

After the war she succumbed to tuberculosis, for she'd never been strong. There followed nine months in a sanatorium, from which she emerged with just one and a quarter lungs.

Polly had always been a writer, and by the time she was 29 she had half a dozen children's books to her name. A dominant memory from my childhood is of Polly bent over a folding card table in the living room, looking through a magnifying glass at photographs of letters, and making copious notes on index cards. She was working on the biography of a bishop, which was published some years later.

But aside from the biography, the demands of domesticity largely put paid to her writing career. She met my father, six years younger than she, and they married and emigrated to South Africa, where I was raised, and where I lived until eventually escaping.

When I was twelve my parents' marriage finally broke down. I say finally, because my father had been serially unfaithful right from the early years of their union. This was particularly difficult for Polly, not least because of my father's occupation. He was a vicar, an Anglican vicar; I suppose you'd have to call him a serially-bonking vicar.

So there were all these parish scandals for poor Polly to deal with, and if there's one kind of scandal you don't want to have to deal with, it's a parish one. The one that finally ended the marriage was a real humdinger. My father decided that he fancied a much younger woman. Much, much younger, in fact. She was only sixteen when they started their affair, just five years older than me. The parish wasn't just shocked, they were scandalized, and my father was defrocked, which is a funny word, but basically just meant he was no longer considered fit to be behind the pulpit, which was probably fair enough.

After the divorce we moved around a lot. When I say we, I mean Polly, my middle brother and I. My oldest brother had left home already. He was the same age as my father's new girlfriend and he'd got out young, finding the atmosphere in the vicarage toxic to say the least.

The years of single parenthood were not easy for Polly, but then the married years hadn't exactly been a bed of roses either. Aside from having to contend with the serial bonking, there'd been very little money. In those days Anglican vicars were paid a pittance, and Polly often went hungry to ensure everyone else had something to eat.

After the very public and scandalous divorce, there were several abortive attempts to settle in the United Kingdom, and eventually came the move to New Zealand. By this time I was in my mid-twenties, and had a two-year-old son, but no husband. (I've never been very good at bagging an andras.) And that's where we stayed more or less, until the start of this adventure. Polly fitted in a few trips back and forth to South Africa, but I had a child at school to consider, and a need to repress my wanderlust for his sake.

In light of this unconventional and unsettled background, it is perhaps not so astonishing that Polly was game for an octogenarian adventure. She was more than game, in fact. Ever since I'd left New Zealand she had been busy, scheming and planning, and getting organized. She had no fears about throwing away everything comfortable and known, and emigrating to a country she'd visited only once on a brief stopover and about which she had a great many romantic and misty misconceptions, and where she knew no one and didn't speak the language. For this was a woman who'd made a life's habit of stepping boldly into the unknown.

But for now I was cycling through the unspectacular outskirts of the village of Methoni. On my right was the usual soccer pitch made of the usual gravel. Every Greek village had a soccer pitch and they always seemed to be made of concrete or gravel. I used to wince just looking at them, for soccer is a sport that involves a fair bit of biting of dust.

To my left were the usual abandoned building sites: villas optimistically begun, but not yet completed. It was not surprising that building works were never completed in Greece. I camped in full view of a building site once, and got to watch Greek building construction in action. A truckload of men would turn up at a reasonable hour, 8 or 9 am, and they'd do a few hours work. Then they'd stop. For about four hours they'd sit in the shade and drink large flagons of local wine. Any work done after that was at best cursory, and then they'd all climb in the truck and go home again.

Here among the new builds, there was also a simple municipal sign, and just reading the name 'Methoni,' I turned cold as ice and was overcome with emotion—and that was just the name, I hadn't even seen the village yet.

But when I did, I was instantly charmed, overwhelmed, besotted, enraptured, and generally head over heels in love. Methoni was gorgeous. I had reached my Utopia. It had narrow little streets, the main one lined with shops, and a gentle hillside dotted with houses in the usual seaside amphitheatre arrangement. The little harbour was charming: there were brightly coloured fishing boats, a calm, flat, shallow bay for swimming, and it had a castle.

I had thought Chlemoutsi Castle in Kastro was something else, and the Castle in Pilos hadn't been too dusty either. But nothing — no castle I had ever seen, or imagined — could have prepared me for the splendour of Methoni Castle.

There was a magic about Methoni Castle — it wasn't just that it was beautiful, it was more than that. It was alive with ghosts, thousands of them. When I slipped inside the Byzantine chapel in the middle of a vast inner field dotted with ruined roundhouses and broken down buildings, I was aware of them. It was a haunted castle. How could it not be haunted with its violent and turbulent history? Suffering wave upon wave of invasions from the sea, first the Venetians, then the Turks, and then the Venetians again, the place saw slaughter upon slaughter. The invading hordes would settle down, have families, and the whole terrible cycle would be repeated a century or so later.

From the day I arrived there, the ghosts of Methoni seemed to wrap themselves around me, demanding that I stay. I tried to leave but I couldn't, and when eventually we did leave it would be because Polly had taken a profound dislike to the ghosts of Methoni, and had embarked on a vigorous and ultimately successful campaign to shake the red dust of the place from her feet from the very day she arrived.

141

It was hard to understand the impact the place had on me. It wasn't the people, that's for sure. The couple in the periptero or kiosk down by the beach were two of the rudest, horridest Greeks I had ever had the misfortune to meet. Every time I went there I swore I would never return, but it was annoyingly convenient, and I returned all too often to patronize their nasty little establishment.

There were some lovely people, of course. There was Katerina in the bakery, and there was a very sweet woman who optimistically ran a bookshop in a town where no-one read. Then there was Yiannis the real estate agent, who wore expensive jewellery and winked and flirted. But I'd met plenty of people in other places that I'd connected with more deeply.

It certainly wasn't the culture or the exciting events that won me over, because nothing at all ever happened there. Every week I would pick up a copy of the Messinian (the free English language newspaper) and scour it for news of something, anything, that might just be happening to alleviate the boredom. There was an artichoke festival in Makromania, a music festival in Pilos, a drama festival in Kalamata, and even a potato festival in Messinia, but in Methoni there was nothing. I'd have given a lot for a bean or aubergine festival to relieve the monotony, but it wasn't to be.

It wasn't the surrounding landscape either. I had seen much more beautiful countryside, the unsurpassable beauty of Kefalonia, for example. Here, in this remote corner of Messinia, it was uninterestingly flat, and the only break in the flatness was the Pilos hills, of which there were four, shaped like breasts. But apart from these four breasted hills there was nothing much to awe the eye. There was the castle of course, but you can't build a life around a ruined castle.

I was not alone in my bewitchment. I met people who had holidayed in Methoni all their lives. Giorgos, who I met in the camping ground, told me that he always cried whenever he rounded that last bend, surmounted that last hill and saw Methoni spread out before him, and he couldn't explain it either.

"You must not write about Methoni," he said. "It's a secret. I do not want people to find out about it."

Sorry Giorgos.

After a couple of weeks living in the municipal camping grounds in Methoni, I woke up one morning, and, ignoring the fact that the inner compass had been quietly content ever since I'd arrived, thought: *this is ridiculous, you can't stay in this place forever.*

So I packed up, signed out of the camping ground, and wheeled my bicycle up through the gaps that had been hewn in the chalky, ochre-coloured hills, determined to leave. But I cried the whole way, and I couldn't understand it. Why was I crying over a little Greek village that I'd only known a few weeks, that was nothing to me, nor I to it?

I had been told there was a night ferry to Crete from Kalamata and I decided I'd catch it, because I had a cousin living on that island who I'd not seen since childhood, and I thought it might be fun to try and find him. I did not realize at that point that Methoni would have very different ideas.

So late in the second afternoon, I found myself in a kafenion alongside Kalamata's ferry office. The ticket office was closed, but the ancients there assured me that was entirely normal. The office would open at 6.30pm for the 10pm sailing, they said.

To while away the time I had a conversation in Greek with one old man who could speak no English, but who managed to understand my Greek better than the rest. He "translated" my Greek into more comprehensible Greek for the benefit of the others. The old men were curious; they wanted to know if New Zealand had the euro and what the fishing was like: the preoccupations of Greece, superimposed upon New Zealand.

A fiery waitress darted among us, haranguing the old men, who gave as good as they got, but 6.30pm came and went. I was not too alarmed at first, this was Greece after all, but at 7.30, and still no signs of life at the ticket office, I became uneasy.

The old men persuaded the fiery waitress to telephone the ferry company to find out what was going on. She appeared to have taken me in dislike, and there was something suspiciously like triumph in her voice when she returned to announce there was no ferry to Crete — not till next Thursday, five days off.

Kalamata, a sprawling, ugly, decentralized town, had no camping site that I knew of, and it was not a good place to be stuck as night fell, especially in light of the ongoing Financial Crisis, and the fact that hotels just weren't in the budget. But the old men assured me there were indeed campsites in Kalamata — two of them — just a couple of kilometers along the beach.

It seemed unlikely from the look of the place, but I wheeled my bicycle in the direction in which they pointed, and there, sure enough, was a sign for a campsite, pointing up a quiet side road. The place was deserted and gloomy, with just a solitary man raking leaves beneath some trees.

I asked him how much it cost to camp for the night. He rubbed his fingers together in a gesture I did not like and said, "Lots of money, because you are a capitalist," which was probably not the best way to win over a client. He named a sum, about average for a campsite, but it wasn't that that bothered me. Aside from not liking that he'd called me a capitalist, since there's lots of rude names that fit me, but that's not one of them, I just had one of those uncomfortable feelings about the place.

Something was saying: *do not pitch your tent here*. It felt unsafe, and not just because it was deserted. I had camped fearlessly in isolated places before. There was something more to it than that, something intangible but real, that filled me with a strong desire to leave.

So I did just that, muttering some feeble excuse as I went. For a woman travelling alone (or indeed anyone travelling alone), such intuitions were beyond important. I always listened to them. If a place or a person made me feel uncomfortable, I left. And this it is, I think, that saved me from meeting the sort of grisly end that Henry had predicted for me, all that time ago, back in the Netherlands.

The second campsite wasn't much better, but at least it didn't feel as if a Greek tragedy was about to be enacted with me as its victim. It was on the main beach-front road, tucked between the tavernas and hotels and within uncomfortably close proximity to a pink discotheque with lurid flashing lights both inside and out. Truly horrible Greek renditions of American and British pop songs kept me awake till all hours the three nights I spent there, while trying to make up my mind whether to catch the ferry to Crete or push on to the Mani peninsula.

I had a slight reason to visit the Mani, not a specially compelling reason, but a reason no less. Friends in New Zealand had put me in touch with a British couple who had built a house in a town called Stoupa. I had a much more compelling reason *not* to visit the Mani, however, because I knew from report it was extremely mountainous and barren with very few campsites, and cycling through it was bound to be tough, especially now that summer was in full force and the daily temperatures were soaring into the high thirties.

The Mani won out over the ferry to Crete, more because I couldn't stand Kalamata another minute than through any shortcomings of Crete, and on the fourth day I set out for Stoupa late in the morning.

This was a grave mistake. It was always advisable to set out as close to dawn as possible. Between Kalamata and Stoupa were mostly mountains, beautiful mountains granted, but mountains nevertheless. The barren, rocky landscape afforded little or no shelter from the sun. The bike ride was broken up into crazed dashes from one roadside olive tree to the next, where I would stand, or sit if there was anywhere to sit, waiting for the drenching rivulets of perspiration to cease. My bottled water was as hot as if it had come straight from a kettle, and the misery of the day was unceasing.

I'd been told there was a campsite at Kardomilia, some kilometers short of Stoupa. The descent to Kardomilia was spectacular—the road coiled, serpent-like, down the mountainside, and it was freewheeling all the way at a frightening speed, hands sore and sweaty from applying the brakes.

Kardomilia was deserted. I headed for the campsite, which was some two kilometers outside the village, according to the directions I'd been given. When I got there all I could see was a deserted patch of land that looked as if it had once been a campsite: those familiar little electricity boxes and the remains of pitches, but there was no campsite, not anymore.

I was exhausted, dejected, ragingly thirsty and incapable of travelling another kilometer. And then, in one of those gifts of Providence that aided me throughout, I chanced on a family running a portable snack bar at the side of the road. They explained that the camping ground had closed years ago, but I was welcome to camp in their olive grove if I liked.

It was from these people that I learned something of the dark side of Greece: the trafficking there of women from Eastern European countries. Each year tens of thousands of women were lured to Greece on the false promise of paid employment in respectable situations. Once there, their passports were stolen, they were kept penniless, and forced into prostitution through violence and threats of violence.

The story, so dark and terrible, told against such a paradisiacal backdrop, and told so matter-of-factly, as if this was just the way things were, and the way things always will be, haunted me. It formed the inspiration, in fact, for my novel *The Incorruptible*, in which the heroine, with the sort of courage that I, her creator, do not possess, bravely takes on the men who are profiting from this evil trade.

There was a campsite on the outskirts of Stoupa, and it was disgusting. Accumulated rubbish lay around in bags for days, attracting thick black swarms of flies of the biting variety. I had not realized until Stoupa that flies could bite. But these ones certainly knew how to bite. Perhaps they'd developed the skill from gnawing their way through the abandoned rubbish bags.

Yet I liked the place enough to stay five days. It was owned and run by a bitter young man called Yiannis. "I have a three million euro property here," he said, "and I take just €100 a day if I am lucky." I refrained from pointing out that if he spent a few of those €100 on a cleaning lady, he might find himself taking more.

It was one of those places you either liked or loathed. I liked it because I was practically alone there. It was deserted in no small part because it was a fly-infested cess-pit, and of course it wasn't in the German Camper's Bible. But apart from the unsanitary conditions it was perfectly fine. The best thing about it was the little private cove where I swam every day, down a hundred or so rough stone steps hewn into the cliff.

Yiannis was bitter about his little cove, too. Yiannis was bitter about everything. "Tourists," he said, although not in quite these words, "want instant gratification. If they cannot step out of their tent or campervan straight into the sea, it just isn't good enough. They are too lazy to climb up and down the steps. And if the beach isn't sandy, well that isn't good enough either. I don't care," he added. "If they can't appreciate what is here, then good riddance to them."

And he rid himself of many a prospective customer, I noticed, in the five days I was there. They would drive in, take one look at the flies, and turn straight round and drive off. But he was a good man. On the wall of his tumble down office he'd painted a giant mural — a stylized rendition of the holy spirit dove. And he allowed me to use the electricity free of charge, so I was able to sit under an olive tree, power up the oldest laptop in the world, which lacked battery as well as wireless capacity of course, and swat away the flies as I wrote.

Finding a supply of electricity for the laptop was one of the leading challenges of my trip. Most campsites charged at least as much for electricity as for the site itself, which was perfectly reasonable if you were driving a large campervan and powering lights, a fridge, air conditioning and a stove.

But if all you needed electricity for was the oldest laptop in the world, it seemed a bit excessive to pay the full rate. Campsites that insisted I pay the full rate were generally campsites where I tended not to linger.

Stoupa itself was horrible, completely ruined by tourists. Even though it wasn't high season yet, already the place was packed to the gills with gently roasting Britons. "It gets much worse," said the friend of a friend I had come to meet. "In August you cannot move on the beach."

We sat in the garden of her magnificent newly built house and in my shabby biking clothes I felt like a poor relation. I had mentioned that I possessed just three changes of clothing in the course of a discussion about the practicalities of cycling and camping, and how difficult that was. And so I found it most odd that when she gave me the tour of the house, she made a point of opening the closet in her bedroom so I could take a good look at all the clothes that were hanging there.

There are people in this world who get a thrill out of boasting about their possessions, I suppose, and apparently she was one of these. Normally I avoid such folk, but I'd not known in advance to do so. I'd travelled a long way to meet these people, without really knowing anything about them, and now all I wanted to do was flee, because they made me feel uncomfortable and inferior, and perhaps that was the intention.

Thus it was that in Stoupa I had a tertiary crisis within the primary crisis. From the moment I'd left Methoni, I'd had a sense of moving in the wrong direction, of travelling down a road that led nowhere. The compass was stirring again, only it wasn't pulling south this time, it was pulling west, drawing me back to Methoni. I had to go back because everything would fall into place there. Which it sort of did. For a while, anyway, before it all turned to custard.

So it was back on the bike to endure the punishing two day ride in a heat wave that was breaking records, even in Greece. The last ten kilometers through the passes cut in the ochre hills were tough beyond description. And then at last I rounded the last curve, topped the final hill, and there it was, spread out before me again — the little amphitheatre of white houses with their orange tile roofs, the bay with its multicoloured fishing boats, and the sprawling castle – glowing warm pinkish grey in the afternoon sunshine. The perspiration was running off me in rivers, but I went ice cold once again at the sight. I stopped the bicycle and stood and gazed at Methoni the Beautiful, my Utopia, my home for the foreseeable future, God willing, or God unwilling, as it turned out.

I had made my decision. I'd find a house or apartment to rent in or near Methoni, and I'd give Polly the go ahead to come and join me. And we would live happily ever after in this exquisitely unspoilt corner of Greece.

Chapter 14: House Hunting in Methoni

Giorgos, my new friend in the camping site in Methoni entered fully into the spirit of house-hunting. He knew everyone in the village, because he'd been holidaying there all his life. He took me round in his little VW beetle, and introduced me to all the potential landlords in town.

There was something unhurried and lovely about the way business was transacted in Greece. We'd call on a family, be taken indoors with great courtesy, and plied with cups of coffee and plates heaped with sweet pastries.

Then would follow a long conversation about everything under the sun, everything except the reason we were there. Eventually Giorgos would broach the subject: *the foreign woman is looking for a house or apartment to rent.*

But it was much more difficult than I'd anticipated. For one thing, it was a bad time of year. Potential landlords were thin on the ground. Much of the available accommodation was given over to holiday lets, and it was now slap bang in the middle of the season, so there were no immediate long-term vacancies. Regular long-term accommodation was in short supply, also, because of the influx of migrant workers from places like Albania and Romania.

But Giorgos was nothing if not determined. He'd promised he would find me somewhere to live, and he refused to give up until he had.

After the first day of house hunting, which was unsuccessful on one level, although I *had* met a lot of lovely people, I cycled into the hills beyond Methoni to a tiny village called Evangelismos some six kilometers distant. The reasoning behind this was that I might be more successful in the kind of place no-one ever went. And no-one ever went to Evangelismos.

The road from Methoni was gentle by Greek standards. I only had to get off the bicycle and push for four of the six kilometers. Halfway there I came across a tiny chapel in the middle of nowhere and sat awhile on the bench outside, admiring the view across the bay of Methoni. Then I went inside and lit a candle and thought *it is because of places such as this that I came to Greece.*

Evangelismos, when I got there, was an ordinary Greek village: a handful of traditional houses, a couple of seedy looking shops, a few seedy looking cafes, and splendid church. The first person I saw moving slowly down one of the narrow streets was leading a donkey. It was, in other words, delightful.

I had been told that the best way to find a place to rent was to visit a kafenion and ask the old men who spent their days there if they knew of anything. So I ordered a coffee and sat down to wait. My time in Greece had taught me that was all I needed to do. I didn't need to initiate a conversation. I just had to wait for natural curiosity to kick in. In a place like Evangelismos, they didn't see too many strangers, so the arrival of a woman on a bicycle was something of an Event.

There were the usual inquiries establishing my non-Germanic origins, and the whereabouts of my andras. Then one of the Ancients, who had spent a year or two in Australia in his youth, was nominated as the Translator for the group. He relayed any difficult bits to the rest of the assembled crowd.

Mention of Polly, and how she would soon be joining me to enjoy the beautiful climate and countryside of Greece went down very well with the Ancients. The elderly are respected in Greece and looking after elderly parents is the rule, not the exception. No doubt there are old people's homes somewhere, but I certainly didn't see any.

They were a lot more dubious about the whole bicycle and tent business. At one point Nominated Translator got up, went to the door, pointed at the bicycle and roared loudly, in tones of triumph : SO WHAT HAPPENS WHEN YOU GET A FLAT TYRE? I told him I fixed it, which was a complete fib, because on the couple of occasions it had happened, I'd found an andras to do it.

The ancient men of the kafenion explained that it was difficult to find a house to rent in Evangelismos. All the old houses were rented by migrant Bulgarian and Albanian workers, they said. But they wanted to help. "Come back in a week," said the Nominated Translator. "I would like to help you."

"I also would like to help you," said another Ancient, who had been silent thus far.

As it turned out, I never went back, because Giorgos visited my tent later that day and told me he'd found me something in Methoni. And that's how I met Kyrie Zacharias, with his three-bedroom apartment that would be available late in August. It wasn't ideal, because it would mean living in the municipal camping ground for another six weeks, and I was already fed up to the back teeth with the municipal camping ground. But it was the first real possibility and so we went, Giorgos and I, to meet Kyrie Zacharias.

We went, I saw it, I liked it very much, and I said yes please. In retrospect, it wasn't that great. But when you've been living in a tent for months, even a garden shed starts to look really luxurious. And there was nothing wrong with it exactly. Okay, it didn't have a living room; there was just an all-purpose eating, cooking and living area, but since that didn't bother me, there was no reason to suppose it would bother Polly either. I mean, why would it?

There were three bedrooms, and the rent seemed very reasonable at €350 a month. It was just fifty or so meters from the castle, and a hundred meters from the beach. When Polly arrived we'd be able to go for walks there together. She had a crumbling spine and couldn't walk very far, but with beach and castle within such easy reach, it would be ideal. And of course Polly was going to love the beach and the castle. It was inconceivable that she wouldn't, and because inconceivable, I didn't conceive it, not for a second.

I had a few misgivings about Kyrie Zacharias, however. He was a short man, with a severe dose of universal short-man syndrome, which, combined with the Greek temperament, indicated the strong possibility of an aggressive character. He'd not done anything to confirm this impression yet, but I could just tell.

So it was agreed, I was to rent the apartment, and I arranged to meet him the following day to pay the first month's rent.

"Come early," said Kyrie Zacharias, although he didn't specify an exact time. What exactly was early in Greece? I had no idea. So I went along after church. Mrs Zacharias had been in church too, and we arrived at the apartment together.

What Kyrie Zacharias had actually meant by early was 'while my wife is in church,' but this I only realized as I watched him going to great lengths to expel her from proceedings. I couldn't follow the conversation but it was clear from the context, gestures, and shouting that this was what was happening. Mrs Zacharias didn't want to be expelled from proceedings, but eventually her husband prevailed, as I suspected he did in most things.

Then, with his wife out of the way, Kyrie Z fetched his neighbor to function as translator. This wasn't very effective because the neighbour's English wasn't any better than my Greek, so it took a while to understand what was going on. It was all starting to seem overly elaborate for what I had thought was going to be the simple handover of a month's rent in advance.

We were sitting at the table in my soon-to-be apartment (soon, but not nearly soon enough) and I extracted the €350 from my money belt and laid it on the table, and Kyrie Zacharias took out his receipt book.

"Kyrie Zacharias is going to give you a receipt for €150," said the neighbour.

"But I thought the rent was €350," I said.

"The rent is €350, but Kyrie Zacharias will give you a receipt for €150," the neighbor insisted.

"No," I said, because I'm a little dense sometimes. "The receipt is for €350."

There was a hurried conference between the neigbour and Kyrie Z of which I understood not a word. The neighbor was looking more and more uncomfortable and it occurred to me I wasn't playing ball properly, but then it's difficult to play ball when you have no idea what the game is, or what the rules are.

At last the neighbor came straight out with it. "If Kyrie Zacharias writes you a receipt for €350, the government tax people will come and steal it."

So Kyrie Z was cooking the books. Of course. I didn't like it overmuch, because I didn't know how the Greek authorities viewed such matters. I didn't fancy the idea of falling foul of the authorities for tax evasion, even if I wasn't profiting personally. I'd seen one too many episodes of Banged Up Abroad.

But I needn't have worried, because from subsequent inquiries I learned that tax evasion is a national past-time in Greece, and one of the reasons the country got itself tied up in so many financial knots. No-one pays tax in Greece, not if they can help it, anyway.

Chapter 15: Bedding down with Serpents

The dodgy deal with Kyrie Z had secured me a spacious and comfortable apartment. No more would I have to sleep, eat and work on the hard ground, no more would I share a tent with the insect population of Methoni, and there'd be no more disgusting communal bathroom block to endure. I'd had enough of all that, and I couldn't wait. But I had to wait, even though the prospect of another six weeks or so in Methoni's municipal camping ground was almost more than I could bear.

As Greek camping grounds went, it wasn't bad at all. It was spacious, well tree'd and it fronted right onto the beautiful beached bay. It was unhygienic enough to deter Germans, and even at the height of the season it was never completely full. But camping grounds were not intended as places to live for more than a couple of weeks at a time, and neither were tents.

I discovered stuff about tents that I'd never have known if I hadn't had to live in one for months on end. The most important thing to know is that they are best suited to a life on the road. You pitch them, sleep in them, unpitch them, shake them out (very important) and head off to the next place. But if you omit these steps, and leave them standing for more than twenty four hours, they become the desirable new home for an entire ecosystem of insects.

As I travelled south through Europe everything got bigger. This applied to nice things like fruit — the nectarines and tomatoes were about six times as large in Greece as they were in Britain for example. But the principle also applied to unpleasant things, like spiders, and worms, and all the other nameless and horrifying insects and arachnids of Greece.

I soon found that if I didn't remove all the contents from my tent at least every other day, unpitch it, give it a good shake and conduct a thorough search of seams, corners and crevices, by the third night I would be wakened by feet running all over me, and sometimes quite large feet. This was not a pleasant sensation in the dark. There was no way of knowing just what it was that was running over me, and my imagination would immediately run riot.

The worst moment would come in the morning, because when conducting the ritual tent-emptying, I would discover exactly who it was that I'd been sharing my bed with. There'd be spiders big as hen's eggs, and a whole host of other creeping and crawling things not designed to charm the human eye. They'd tumble out and creep and crawl off through the grass, to bide their time, before returning later when they'd bring their friends and family with them.

Worst of all were the snakes. Greece had two species of common snake — there were the thin ones and there were the fat ones. The fat ones grew up to four meters, and they were bright green, and looked incredibly frightening. The first time I saw one it was in the process of exiting my tent, but fortunately I wasn't in my tent at the time.

I was assured that the fat ones were harmless. They would run, or rather slither away, rather than confront a human being. The thin ones were a different matter. They were black and sinister-looking, and would not baulk at a confrontation. They would go on the offensive if they found themselves in a situation they considered threatening: a situation such as sharing a tent with a screaming woman in a municipal camping ground in Methoni.

I awoke in the middle of one night and saw quite clearly the shadowy shape of a snake, about a foot and a half in length, making its way along the side of the tent beside me. It was one of the thin ones.

So there I was, in the middle of the night, in the pitchy dark, outside my tent, having exited more quickly and more screechily than ever before, and with no intention whatsoever of going back inside till morning. It was a long night spent sitting on a rock at a suitable distance, listening to the sound of frogs singing.

At dawn I unpitched very gingerly, and shook the contents out onto the grass. I didn't see it go; it must have left before then, but it was a long time before I slept easy after that.

There were pleasant aspects to living so close to nature, of course, and these included the birds. The almost tame sparrows were a delight, even if they did crap constantly onto my tent from the trees above. So as well as the ritual tent emptying, the ritual tent washing became part of my daily routine.

I shared many a meal with the sparrows of Methoni. They'd hop excitedly about at mealtimes and some would even take crumbs from my hand. The doves were glorious, too — they started cooing at dawn, and it was one of the sounds I came to associate with Greece, the land of doves cooing.

Aside from the wildlife, from which there was no escape, there were many other trials to be borne those two long months spent in the municipal camping grounds of Methoni. It was, for example, not easy trying to write out of doors when the temperature was soaring into the forties. The sun was constantly on the move, and my days were spent chasing ever-vanishing patches of shade beneath trees. Preventing rivers of sweat dripping onto the oldest laptop in the world was one of the more difficult challenges of writing out of doors without the benefit of air conditioning.

And I was writing constantly, furiously, all day long, as if my life depended on it, in a desperate attempt to solve the financial problems that were always there, always distracting me, and always taking the gloss off what might otherwise have been an enchanted time.

I was down to just a few hundred dollars by this time, having spent the last large chunk of my funds on that first month's rent on the apartment that was not yet mine. And in the meanwhile I had to pay the campsite for the privilege of living with snakes and spiders, and I had to eat. And I had to feed the dog, yes, the dog, but more about him later.

Food was a constant issue. Aside from the obvious fact that food costs money, and as noted, I didn't have a lot of it, the municipal camping ground in Methoni did not have refrigerators. Granted, only the better camping grounds did, but again this was a trial that was more bearable when on the move. It was another matter when making any kind of prolonged stay in a place. There were a couple of freezers dotted about the grounds, and these were good for cooling down water and some other necessities, but were hopeless for fruit, vegetables, cheese, yoghurt, and all the other myriad products that spoil if frozen, but that spoil even faster in forty degree temperatures.

So I was forced to calculate my daily purchases down to the last mouthful, and even then there was waste. Furthermore, in Greece as most everywhere else, food bought in tiny quantities is infinitely more expensive than food bought in bulk. So along with longing for a proper bed, I endured my exile in Methoni Camping ground dreaming of the large refrigerator I'd seen in Kyrie Z's apartment.

Then there was the little matter of the public conveniences, which weren't particularly convenient, but were certainly public. All the windows were either broken or missing and none of the doors closed properly. This made showering and going to the loo quite a challenge. I had to crouch down in the shower, so that families of happy campers, with their innocent children, weren't treated to an unwelcome eyeful. It would have been peeping tom paradise, but after a while I learned not to worry too much about that.

Perhaps the worst of the trials to be borne were the hordes of happy holidaymakers, hordes that increased in numbers when July rolled into August. I'd had the place almost to myself in the beginning, and had chosen a remote spot far away from anyone else, and this I had enjoyed for weeks on end. But the peace was disrupted, as peace always is, and the disruption took the form of a vast French family, their enormous campervan, their six bedroom tent and their three cats.

I watched in amazement as the cats emerged, one by one, wearing harnesses and leads, to be taken for a sedate promenade around the campsite. The woman told me they'd made the decision to bring the cats on their annual holiday because one year they'd returned home to a dead cat. Whoever had been caring for it hadn't done a very good job. This had traumatized the family so badly they'd decided taking the cats with them was the best solution.

That the cats didn't agree was glaringly obvious. They didn't like Methoni municipal camping grounds one bit. I could tell from the way their tails were swishing that they thought going for walks on leads a terrible idea. It was, I think, something to do with the indignity of being treated like dogs.

Which brings me back to the dog: on the first night of my return to Methoni after the unsuccessful excursion to the Mani Peninsula, I had woken in the morning to find a large, shaggy, and not terribly attractive dog lying outside my tent. After some initial alarm I realized he was one of the friendly ones, and then he took a great liking to me, something that was in part my own fault.

Because when he said *where's breakfast?* I made a decision that had lasting consequences. I fed him. He was nothing but trouble from that moment on. He would disappear after breakfast, and then he'd come back in the middle of the night, stand outside my tent and bark loudly. The only way I could get him to shut up was to let him inside. So there I was, sharing my tent not only with the insect population of Methoni, but with an ugly, hairy, and very smelly Greek dog.

He turned up one morning injured. He'd gone and got himself shot, presumably by being a nuisance somewhere he wasn't appreciated. He dragged his poor wounded self—one of his rear legs a mess of embedded shotgun pellets— underneath the caravan of a family of horrified Italians, and we had to get Methoni's version of the RSPCA to come and take him away.

I have to admit that I was relieved. Not that he'd been shot, but that he'd gone, because he was a first rate nuisance. They will fix him up, I thought, find him a nice home and I won't be woken up in the middle of the night again. But it was not that simple.

In Greece they merely treated wounded animals and then set them free again, so he turned up again, about a week later, in the middle of the night, barking joyfully and saying *where's breakfast.*

My new French neighbor, who'd arrived in the period of peace while the dog was in doggie hospital, came flying out of his campervan to rescue me. It was nice of him, I suppose, but it took a while to convince him I was not being attacked, and simply greeted with joy. When he realized the dog and I were friends, he turned from chivalrous Frenchman to angry Frenchman in the blink of an eye, and made it very clear he thought the dog was all my fault, and being woken up in the middle of the night was my fault also.

So in the morning I moved myself to the furthest remaining remote corner of the campground, where the dog would be a menace only to myself.

The brightest spot in this rather trying period spent waiting for the apartment, was the discovery of a book exchange, hidden away in one of the twisty back streets of the village. A Dutch couple, who'd bought a house in the area, had decided that they'd also start up a business catering to expats and tourists. They didn't as yet have a license to operate, for they'd run into all the usual problems with Greek bureaucracy, and so were operating surreptitiously.

It felt a bit like buying bootleg brandy during Prohibition. I had to knock on a door veiled with curtains, and then we conducted our business secretly. The transaction culminated in my departure with a brown paper bag containing my illicit copy of Huckleberry Finn.

Because they were Dutch, most of the books were in Dutch, and they were surely limiting themselves in this decision, because the Dutch population in the village consisted of just two — themselves — but they did have one bookcase of English books.

I'd been starved of reading matter for months, and was surprised just how much I missed it. I became ravenously hungry for the English language, to hear it, to speak it, and most of all, to read it. I can understand why people who move abroad in their retirement, to Spain or France, say, full of high hopes of a new life in the sun, give up and flee home to the grey skies of England or Wales, especially if they've moved somewhere English is little-spoken, and where they don't speak the language.

Mark Twain's Huckleberry Finn was the first English book I'd read since I left New Zealand. I felt like a starving woman at a banquet. I savoured every word, and I read it at a snail's pace. I usually devour books at great speed, but I never wanted Huckleberry Finn to end. It seemed like the greatest book that had ever been written in the whole world, and who knows, maybe it is.

Alas, my reading matter for the next couple of weeks was to be sorely circumscribed by what was there. I worked my way through the decent stuff in no time at all, and then all that was left was Dan Brown and Jack Higgins.

Chapter 16: "I am too busy to sell you a telephone"

The glorious day had arrived. It was moving day, although to call it moving day is stretching it a bit. It was the day I got to pack up the now hated tent, my pannier bags of worn out gear, and cycle a kilometer along the beach to my wonderful apartment, where I'd sleep on a bed for the first time in months, where I'd shower in a bathroom that didn't have a broken window, and where I'd eat my food at a real table, instead of on the hard ground, surrounded by ants and sparrows and giant Greek flies.

Best of all, I'd be able to stop enriching the man in the internet café with €5 an hour to use a computer. I'd be able to get a phone line, and an internet connection, and how much easier it would be to hustle for work, send off articles, and communicate with friends and family, in particular with Polly, who was now readying herself in the wings to step onto the Greek stage that awaited her.

The apartment was on one of Methoni's two main streets. The other main street was where the shops were, all ten of them, and this, the second main street was narrow, but also quite busy.

I was often woken in the middle of the night by late summer revellers passing the window. Opposite the apartment was one of Methoni's three village squares, with the usual pavement cafes and bars, and that too could get quite noisy at night.

The apartment itself was simple, but adequate. I did have to spend a disproportionate amount of time with broom and mop, because the white-tiled floors showed every grain of red sand that blew in constantly from North Africa. But apart from that minor disadvantage, it was a pleasant place to live. Or so I thought.

There was one other disadvantage, and that was Kyrie Zacharias. He and his wife lived in the apartment directly above, and all my earlier misgivings about him were soon amply justified.

I don't know if it was a Greek thing, or just a Kyrie Z thing, but he didn't seem at all familiar with what I had previously assumed to be a global requirement for landlords to respect the privacy of their tenants. He'd bang on the door, and when I opened it, he would quite literally push past me and march inside. Once in, he'd do a spot check, poking his nose into the bedrooms, checking the bathroom, opening the fridge. And he'd shout things, but as I had no idea what he was shouting, it was all quite disturbing and not at all welcome.

Still, I'd survived sharing a tent with the uninvited insect population of Greece, an uninvited stray dog and uninvited snakes, so while sharing the apartment periodically with the uninvited Kyrie Z was not something I particularly liked, things had been worse.

The day after I moved in, I caught the bus to the village of Pilos, 10 km away, because Pilos was the nearest town with an OTE office and OTE was Greece's version of Telecom, only far worse.

I was excited and full of hope, and it did not occur to me that an internet connection would be a difficult matter to arrange. In New Zealand if I wanted an internet connection, I'd ring up Telecom, put in the request, and someone would say, "Certainly Madam, your connection will be up and running within an hour." Why should it be any different in Greece?

Pilos was an attractive town, with a small harbour, and shops arranged around a main waterfront square. It was larger and busier than Methoni, for it boasted a hospital, a high-school and a lot more shops. And of course it too had a castle, the castle where I'd kept the custodian waiting a full hour.

In spite of the undeniable charms of the place, I preferred Methoni. For one thing Pilos was far more touristy, and this in part because of its proximity to Navarino Bay, where the naval Battle of Navarino had taken place on 20 October 1827, as part of the Greek War of Independence against the Ottoman Empire, and where it's still possible to see the wrecks littering the sea bed on a sunny day.

The man in the OTE office in Pilos did not speak much English, and did not seem particularly happy to see me. But he managed to say, in response to my request for a telephone connection: "You are needing a tax number before you can have a telephone..."

So it was off to the tax office, which took some effort to find, and even more effort to communicate my need for a tax number. A basic bureaucratic vocabulary was a necessity for life in Greece, and one that I was lacking. One of the main reasons I'd left New Zealand had been to escape bureaucracy, but it had been naïve indeed to think that Greece would be any better in that regard.

"Come back tomorrow for your tax number," said the lady in the tax office, after I had run around Pilos for an hour, trying to find somewhere to photocopy my passport and someone to help me fill out the ridiculously complicated forms requiring information about the last three generations of my family.

Next day I returned to the tax office in Pilos to pick up my tax number, and to visit the man in the OTE office. Again he was not happy to see me and unimpressed with my tax number.

"I am very busy," he said, turning his back on me and not looking at all busy. "You are calling 134 to apply for a telephone connection."

I found out subsequently he could quite easily have done it all for me on the spot, and saved me endless bother, but saving people endless bother was not what he did. So I called 134 as instructed, and made a verbal application for a telephone and internet connection.

"It is not possible to apply for an internet connection until you have a telephone connection," I was told. "But if you call back in three days, we will give you your new telephone number."

It took seven days, in fact. I was eventually given my new number, but there was still no connection. "Ring the technician in Pilos and he will come out and fix the connection."

My heart sank. Requiring the cooperation of anyone at all in the OTE office in Pilos was very bad news. It took three days to get through to the technician in Pilos. I had to catch him very early, before he set off for the day to do goodness knows what, although I doubt it was connecting telephones.

"You must be coming to Pilos to do papers first," he told me. "I cannot connect you until you have done papers."

No-one had mentioned the requirement to do papers before. I begged and pleaded, but to no avail. So it was back to Pilos on the bus, and back to my friend in the OTE office to do papers. He did not look at all happy to see me. It took half an hour to persuade him to do papers and then at least another hour to do them, and then he said: "You must call the technician tomorrow and he will make the connection."

I left the OTE office feeling I had made progress, although none too happy about having to ring the technician again. Then it occurred to me that I should perhaps purchase an actual physical telephone. There wasn't one in the apartment, and I could just imagine the technician turning up at last and saying "You don't have a telephone, so I cannot connect you," and disappearing for another four weeks. I had seen a relatively cheap model in the display cabinet at the OTE office, and so I retraced my steps.

The man in the OTE office was very displeased to see me back so soon. I told him I would like to buy a telephone and pointed to the model I'd chosen.

"I am far too busy to sell you a telephone," he said. "Come back tomorrow morning."

I just couldn't face it. There were only two buses to and from Methoni and Pilos daily, and if I went in on the morning bus, I had to hang around the best part of the day for the bus home. My bicycle was out of action with a puncture I just couldn't seem to get the better of, and besides, I'd had enough of my bicycle.

So I begged the wretched man to sell me the telephone, and when that didn't work I did a sit in. He finally realized I wasn't going away until he sold it to me, so with much huffing and puffing and exaggerated effort, he arose from his desk and did so. It took half an hour to "do papers" connected to selling me a telephone. What sort of country makes you fill out twenty forms to buy a simple telephone?

The telephone itself was completely useless without a connection of course, but at least I had a useless telephone, and had done plenty of papers.

With renewed hope I rang the technician from a callbox next morning. "You are not in my computer," he said. "I cannot connect you until you are in my computer. I will ring you when you are in my computer."

By this point it seemed a waste of energy pointing out that I did not yet have a phone and that I was calling from a call box.

I rang him the next day. And the next. On the third day he grudgingly agreed to come to Methoni the following Friday. He was about to hang up, when I asked him if he knew where I lived. "No," he said.

After much miscommunication and shouting (the shouting was done by him), we finally arranged to meet at the post office at 8.30am next Friday. Much to my surprise he turned up, and within minutes I had a telephone.

I didn't actually want a telephone. The whole and sole point of all this was an internet connection. The telephone was just a means to that end.

"You must go back to the office in Pilos to apply for an internet connection," the technician told me.

The man in the OTE office in Pilos looked very unhappy to see me. "I have come to apply for an internet connection for my telephone," I told him.

"You must be ringing 134 to apply for an internet connection..." he said.

Chapter 17: The Wrong Shade of Yellow

So there I was, living in my three bedroom apartment in Utopia. I finally had the long-awaited, hard-won internet connection; my son Michael was coming to visit soon, and Polly had booked her flight.

"I'll be there in the middle of October," she wrote. "It will be so wonderful. I just can't wait to see you. There are one or two boxes on their way in the post..."

It was just weeks away and I was very excited. It felt as if a void that had been opened up in my life would soon be filled again. Because the truth of the matter was, I'd spent most of my adult life to that point looking after people. I'd raised Michael and I'd also looked after Polly on and off over the years, but now I had no-one to run round after, and I missed it dreadfully. It is a common phenomenon, I believe. A person who has been needed by others for years can find not-being-needed a quite devastating shock and life can suddenly seem empty.

That's how my life in Greece had begun to feel. In the early months of my midlife crisis adventure I'd felt liberated. It was wonderful not to have to look after anyone, not to be needed.

But gradually I'd discovered that freedom wasn't all it was cracked up to be. With Polly there I'd be forced to make meals, cups of tea, and hot water bottles all day long, and that was just fine. I needed Polly as much as she needed me.

She had a catalogue of ailments that would take pages to chronicle. Included among these was a crumbling spine, a most unpleasant condition that caused her a great deal of pain. She also had arthritis of the spine, which meant that even when the crumbling spine wasn't crumbling there was no respite from back pain. As if that wasn't enough she had diabetes, a hiatus hernia, a spastic colon, acid reflux and high blood pressure.

She was nevertheless remarkably good at getting things done, considering the parlous state of her health. Undeterred by her frailty, she gathered about her the usual team of willing and unwilling helpers, and got them packing sorting, disposing, and purchasing on her behalf, in readiness for her great Greek adventure.

This was one of the many admirable qualities about Polly, and also one of the many ways in which she and I were very different. She had an amazing ability to build support groups wherever she went, an army of people she'd get to do stuff. She was never too proud to ask for help.

There were always one or two men numbered in her army, because Polly was of the opinion that men had their uses and you needed to keep a few tame ones on hand in case anything needed fixing. Throughout the periods of our life that were spent together, whenever something went wrong, and something mechanical or electrical needed fixing, Polly's first reaction was always to say to me: "Go find a man…"

She was oblivious to the fact that most men were just as incapable as the average woman of solving practical problems, and had to her death a touching faith in the ability of the male sex to fix things. (That is why God had put them on earth, after all.)

So she managed all the many preparations necessary for moving continents, mostly by telling other people what to do, and glad I was that I wasn't there, very glad, because I'd have been conscripted into the army, too.

This large contingent of friends, both in and outside the old people's internment camp, were sharply divided about her decision to up stakes and move to Greece. There were the nay-sayers and prophets of doom, and there were the please-take-me-with-yous. But Polly had never been one to be swayed by prophets of doom.

Those one or two boxes she'd mentioned turned out to be closer to one or two dozen. They arrived daily through the complicated, but ultimately reliable Greek postal system, and they contained papers, books, manuscripts and photographs. But this was just the tip of Polly's enormous iceberg. She'd be bringing the rest of it with her.

The Greek postal system was a source of wonder, for there were no street names and there were no street numbers. You just addressed your letter or parcel to John Doe, Methoni, Greece, and trusted it would arrive. There were also no letter-boxes or letter flaps in doors, which meant the postman always had to knock, so if there was one person you got to know really well, it was the postman, and the postman in Methoni was a lovely man, and for that I can personally vouch.

At last the big day arrived, a lovely day, with not a cloud in sight to warn of the storm to come. I made the arduous trip to meet Polly in Athens. First there was a bus to Kalamata, and then a coach across the peninsula. It was midnight when I arrived in the capital, where, because I was still watching pennies, I took a bus to Eleftherios Venezelos airport, and spent the night on a plastic bucket seat, waiting for morning, an experience only marginally less trying than the night spent on Genoa station.

Polly's flight landed shortly after dawn, and I watched with tears in my eyes as her entourage came towards me. A solicitous flight attendant was pushing the wheelchair containing the tiny, deceptively frail figure that was Polly. Behind her there was a second flight attendant, wheeling a veritable mountain of luggage, and I realized with horror it was all hers. There were three suitcases, a flight bag, a handbag, a string bag, a plastic bag full of books (airplane reading), a camera bag, a hot water bottle (for her back) a typewriter case, a makeup case, several blankets (in case it was cold on the plane), a pillow (for her back on the plane), and a medicine chest.

The medicine chest contained a year's supply of drugs that she'd managed to persuade some or other representative of the ordinarily anal New Zealand medical fraternity to give her. Among these was a very powerful opiate that she took for her crumbling spine pain, and it was banned in countries all over the world. How she got through customs with that little lot, I will never know. And how she got through without having to pay a king's ransom in excess baggage, I will never know either. Actually that's not true. I do know. Polly just expected people to do things for her, and that applied to the folk at airport check-in counters as much as it did to anyone else. And it is a law of nature that if you simply expect people to do things, more often than not, they oblige.

It was lovely to see her, and I could see that she hadn't changed a bit. Perhaps it would have all worked out better if she had. Perhaps that was the problem. Polly was still Polly; she hadn't miraculously morphed into someone who was suddenly going to be accommodating and pliable.

Looking back, I must have been naïve or crazy to think that Polly could ever be transplanted effortlessly into Greece. I genuinely thought she'd love it at least as much as I did, although I did have one or two minor qualms. I wasn't sure, for example, how she'd handle the Toilet Issue, but they really were very minor qualms.

"It's so lovely to see you darling," she said, introducing me to her two serfs as if she'd known them all her life. That's what Polly was like with people. People she'd known five minutes became as familiar as old friends in an instant. She'd find out all about them, their families, their lives, win them over by appearing interested, and then before they knew it they'd be enlisted in her army. She genuinely was interested, too. It wasn't an act. But there was a certain pragmatism driving it. Polly had learned how best to survive in this world. These particular two serfs were now smiling at her besottedly and calling her 'Mum.'

The warning signs that our Greek idyll was about to be horribly derailed were there right from the beginning. Her beams and smiles started to fade after just half an hour.

"This is nothing like I remember it," she commented ominously as we drove through the outskirts of Athens on some rattletrap bus, after taking up the commodious racks set aside for everyone's luggage single handed, and forcing everyone else to pile theirs up in the aisle.

She went even more ominously silent once we'd entered Athens proper, and the grubby buildings flashed by. It was starting to dawn on me that the celebrated stopover she'd made decades before had centered almost exclusively on the Plaka and the Acropolis, and that was how Polly now thought of Greece. She had reinvented Greece into one giant Athenian Plaka, and the trouble with that was it existed only in her imagination. As anyone who's ever been there knows, most of Greece is nothing like the Plaka, with its quaint souvenir ships, its whitewashed alleyways, its old buildings, its charming tavernas.

When we got to Athens central bus station I managed to secure a taxi to take us to our hotel, but not without difficulty. Athenian taxi drivers have a quite unique attitude to the business of taxiing. If they don't like the look of the job (and in our case they didn't, thanks to the iceberg of luggage), they simply say: 'I'm going the other way.'

I had lived all my life under the mistaken impression that taxi drivers go where passengers want to go, and that it's not up to passengers to find taxis that just so happen to be going their way. But this was Greece, and by then I was used to Greece. Polly, on the other hand, was not.

She didn't like the hotel, but because it had a fully functioning lavatory, I didn't think it necessary to bring up the Toilet Issue just yet. There'd be time enough for that on the morrow, when she'd recovered from the rigours of her journey.

175

The next morning did not start well, because Polly took an instant dislike to the landscape of Greece. Now that's the thing about a landscape—you either like it or you don't. I am not a great fan of the landscape of Wales, for example, because it is the wrong shade of green. This is because of that other thing I don't like about Wales—the over-abundance of water that falls from the sky.

I thought Polly would love the Greek landscape, because she'd loved the South African one, and I didn't think them too different. They were both a sort of khaki colour, parched and rocky, with the kind of vegetation that has learned to live without a great deal of water.

But she didn't like it. She hated it and said she found it depressing. I suppose the surprising thing was not so much that she didn't like it, but that I had not seen this coming and neither had she.

We should have done, because in all our shared life, we'd never once liked the same things. We liked different kinds of books, different kinds of food, of movies, of music, of art. What made us think for one moment that we'd like the same countries? So different were we, she sometimes used to quip that if she didn't quite distinctly remember giving birth to me, she'd be tempted to think I wasn't hers at all. Only because it been a home birth could she rule out the possibility the midwife had made a mistake.

In the matter of food, books, music and movies, this incompatibility was easily remedied. But now the situation was a lot more serious. Here she was, already regretting her decision to move to Greece, and it was only day two. There wasn't a lot either of us could do about it. The bridges were burnt. She couldn't just turn round and go back to New Zealand. She'd given up her place in the retirement home, she'd transferred her pension, she'd come on a one way ticket. There was no going back.

It was one of those cold hollow feeling in the pit of the stomach days, for both of us, as we watched the countryside of Greece going by the windows of our Athens-Kalamata coach, with me thinking, I love it, it's so beautiful, what is wrong with this woman, and her thinking I hate it, it's awful, I've been tricked, I want to go home.

I still had a glimmer of hope, and so too, I think, did she. We were heading, after all, for Methoni the Beautiful, and I'd been raving about Methoni in my emails for several months.

At last we were there, the taxi pulling up outside the apartment, her luggage disgorged. And then, when we'd got it all inside, I led her into the kitchen/living room/dining room and put the kettle on for a much needed cup of tea.

She took a long look around the kitchen

"Where's the living room?" she asked.

"Well, technically there isn't one," I said. "This is it— kitchen, dining room and living room combined."

"I see," she said.

"Where's the bathroom?"

"Here it is," I said, showing her. "But there's something I need to tell you before you use it."

"Oh yes?" she said, in that ominous 'I'm not going to like what's coming' tone of hers.

"Traditional Greek plumbing is a little different from what we are used to. It's not quite so efficient. So we aren't allowed to flush toilet paper down the lavatory. You have to use this little waste bin for that. See, it's got a bin liner, and so it's not a big deal. I replace the bin liner daily, you don't have to bother with it."

Polly turned pale as a ghost. "No," she said, staring at me in horror. "Tell me you are joking."

"I am not joking," I said. "But it's really not a big deal. You'll be surprised how quickly you'll get used to it."

177

"I will *never* get used to it," she said. "Why didn't you tell me about this before? I would *never, ever* have come to Greece, not in a million years, if I had known about this."

It was my turn to stare in horror, unable to believe she wasn't joking. But she wasn't. She was deadly serious. Sure it was a little distasteful, but seeing it was me who'd be dealing with the distasteful aspects and not her, I couldn't really see what all the fuss was about.

"I didn't tell you before because I didn't think it was that significant."

"Of course it's significant," said Polly. "I've never heard anything so disgusting in all my life."

And this from a woman who'd lived through World War II, had lived in abject poverty while my father went to theological college; this from a woman who never had two pennies to rub together, but had somehow managed to live on three continents, and never on any of them for more than five years at a stretch.

But it was no good. I knew our life in Greece was doomed from that moment on. She wouldn't adapt, she'd never get used to it.

She was just too old to make that kind of adjustment. It was a very small adjustment in the greater scheme of things, but I guess at 80, a person has won the right to dig their heels in and refuse to adapt in matters of principle.

The worst thing about the Toilet Issue was that it set her resolutely against everything else. While she'd not been favourably disposed to Greece right from the get-go, now it was as if everything else about Greece that I showed her had to overcome an almost insuperable barrier of Toilet Issue prejudice.

The next morning, when she'd recovered a bit, we went for a walk to the beautiful little bay and sat on a bench there and watched the gentle waves rippling up the unspoilt golden beach. It was a beautiful place, with its multicoloured fishing boats bobbing along the jetty, the waterside tavernas, the blue, blue sky. To our right, there was the magnificent Methoni Castle.

"Isn't it lovely?" I said.

She sat a while in silence. At last she spoke. "I don't like it," she said.

"Why not? What's wrong with it?"

"It's the wrong shade of yellow," she said.

"I beg your pardon?"

"The beach — look at it — it's all wrong, it's too yellow."

"How can a beach be too yellow? It's beautiful!"

But she dug her heels in and was adamant. "I don't like it," she insisted. "It's the wrong colour."

Oh well, I thought, never mind. She will love the castle. That will bring her round. Everyone loves the castle. It's the most astonishing place in the whole of Greece. In our email correspondence she'd said often how much she was looking forward to seeing it. She had a real feeling for history, had Polly, and the thought of the castle had excited her from afar. The castle might even serve to redeem Greek toilets and beaches that were the wrong shade of yellow. So as soon as she was up to it, we visited the Castle.

"It gives me the creeps," said Polly. "I hate it. It's haunted. Get me out of here. I can hear the women weeping and the men crying out. I can see the invading armies. I can sense the bloodshed and the tragedy. I can't stand it in here another second. It's the worst place I've ever been in my life."

Normally it was me with the overactive imagination. I was the one who felt the presence of ghosts, and dreamed vividly every night. Now it was Polly, infinitely more down to earth, and who used to complain she'd never had a dream her entire life, seeing and hearing things.

So much for Methoni Castle. But I had one trump card left and that was the food. Polly was very, very fond of food. And since most people agree that Greek food is glorious, this surely would be the thing to turn everything around and win her over.

"I don't like it," said Polly. "Greek food is horrible. The marmalade is too sweet, the tea is too weak, the coffee is too bitter, the potatoes are too floury, the tomatoes are too juicy, the olive oil makes my stomach run and Greek brandy is not at all as I remember it. I can't eat baklava anymore because I have developed an allergy to nuts. I had forgotten it had nuts. I want English food. I want fish and chips and steak and kidney pie and I want Tetley's tea bags."

What shall I do, I wailed to God. *What shall I do?*

And then God revealed His true colours; that he wasn't on my side after all. He was on Polly's side. I do not interpret this to mean that God shared Polly's opinion of Greece, far from it. It was just that Polly's prayers, which were tending in the opposite direction from mine, appeared to carry far more weight with the Almighty.

My proofreading work dried up overnight. I went from having just enough work to having no work at all. It was mysterious, and not a little alarming. I needed an income. There was no local work, either, aside from seasonal jobs in cafés and bars, and we were heading into autumn, when such things ceased entirely. I would have been ill-suited to that sort of work, anyway. But I needed to earn money, and it seemed all the doors were banging firmly shut in Greece.

Then came an unexpected email from my brother in Scotland. "Bring Mum to Scotland," he wrote. "I'll help you look after her and you can get a job in the call centre here in Aviemore. They're always looking for people."

Of course they were always looking for people. That's because jobs in call centres are horrible, and no one could stand this particular call centre job much more than a month. They'd already got through all the inhabitants of the Highlands. Even my brother had worked there for a couple of months once and if it was that great, why had *he* left?

There was no way I was going to Scotland. No way at all. I hadn't exchanged a place I considered too cold (Wellington, New Zealand), for the glorious climate of Greece, only to end up within spitting distance of the Arctic Circle in the northernmost Highlands of Scotland.

"I've *always* wanted to go to Scotland," said Polly. "Scotland will be lovely. They have toilets that flush properly, and English food."

"No they don't, they have Scottish food."

"English, Scottish, same thing," said Polly.

"I am not going to work in a call centre," I said, "and that's the only work going in Aviemore. I am going to find work in England or Wales. You shall have your Tetley's tea bags, but we aren't going to Scotland."

Since anywhere at all was better than Greece as far as she was concerned, Polly agreed. Thus began a long and fruitless search for work in England or Wales. There wasn't much I was qualified to do. I had the most useless doctorate in the world (in religious studies), a background in journalism (buried in the mists of time), and during that brief stint in the Ministry of Human Misery, I'd not exactly covered myself in glory, and would struggle to find anyone willing to give me a decent reference.

"I shall teach Religious Studies in a posh school where you don't have to have one of those teaching diploma things," I said. "It will be somewhere rural and pretty and we can rent a cottage with ivy and climbing roses on it."

"But you hate teaching," said Polly.

It was true, I did hate teaching. I'd been a tutor in a religious studies department for years, while writing the most useless doctorate in the world, and I'd hated every minute of it.

"It will be different teaching children," I said, ignoring the deep down conviction it would probably be a whole lot worse.

But I nevertheless wrote to every posh school in England and Wales, informing them all about myself and my PhD in Religious Studies, saying no, I had not taught in a school before, but I'd taught Sunday School once, and I'd taught in a university. And yes, while right now I was living the life of an unemployed gypsy in Greece, I would be back in the United Kingdom soon, and I looked forward to hearing from them...

Not one single posh school bothered to reply, and I wrote to them all. And we couldn't just turn up in some random corner of England or Wales because we had nowhere to live and I didn't have a job. It's impossible to find somewhere to rent from a distance of thousands of kilometers, especially when you don't have a job and you don't have references from previous landlords (see below), and I know this because I tried very hard.

We'd done it once before, Polly and I, when I'd been younger and pregnant with Michael. We'd moved to the United Kingdom together with no idea where we were going. So we closed our eyes, stuck a pin in a map, and it landed near Cardiff. That's where we spent two years and where Michael was born — in Newport, Gwent, to be precise, but that's a whole other story and also a cautionary tale against putting pins in maps. Neither of us was willing to do that again.

What shall we do? I said to God. *Whatever shall we do?*

And God didn't mess about. There was another email from my brother, who appeared to have morphed into God's emissary, at least for the moment. "I've found you a flat," he wrote, "in Aviemore. It's just down the road from me. The landlord says you can have it from the first of February and he isn't even asking for references."

That clinched it. The matter of references was no small matter. In a brief confession, which is said to be good for the soul, I have to admit that along with various other past sins, there was the Landlord Thing. My usual means of departing a property was to just pack up, pop the keys in an envelope and post them to the landlord as I drove away. I'd make sure by the time he or she got the letter, I was long gone. It was just so much less *complicated* that way. If you did the thing properly there were all those nasty encounters. The landlord/lady would come round, eyes darting like snakes everywhere, spotting little marks and splotches and burn holes in the carpet from fifty paces. And then they'd refuse to return the deposit anyway.

But the flip side of taking the easy way out was a long trail of previous residences and not a single reference produced from any of them.

"Right," I said to Polly. "You win. God wins. Brother wins. We're going to Scotland in January. I'll find something else to do, though, because there's no way I'm going to work in that call centre."

"No, darling," said Polly, "I quite agree. It wouldn't suit you at all."

She was all agreeableness now that she'd got her own way, and even stopped complaining about Greek marmalade.

Chapter 18: Doing a Moonlit Flit.

Christmas in Methoni was wonderful, so wonderful even Polly enjoyed it. My son Michael was there, spending it with us, and I will look back on it as one of the best Christmases of my life. This was in no small measure due to the fact that Greeks didn't do Christmas. There was no proliferation of rubbish in the shops, no pressure to spend money on things no-one wanted or needed.

Christmas in Greece was about going to church, eating something nice, and watching one or two religious processions, where the mouldering remains of some or other saint were held aloft in a little glass case, while everyone sang Greek carols. That the sacred relic was more than likely the clavicle of a wild pig or something was irrelevant.

Christmas seemed to bring out the best in everyone. Even the dreaded Kyrie Z was filled with the Christmas spirit, and sent Mrs Z down with a plate of Greek Christmas biscuits.

Shortly after Christmas Michael left, making sure he got out early before preparations for the traumatic exodus to Scotland began in earnest. He's always been clever like that, has Michael, knowing the precise moment it is sensible to get out of the way.

Leaving Greece was going to be a whole lot more difficult than entering Greece had been. This time I had an 80 year old lady to worry about, an elderly lady quite undeserving of the award Travel Companion of the Year, and an awful, awful lot of stuff.

And of course there was the Landlord Thing. Polly, who knew me only too well, sniffed it out early.

"It's three weeks till we leave," she said. "When are you going to tell Kyrie Zacharias we're going?"

"Soon," I said, "soon."

She repeated the question every day for four days. And then she said accusingly: "You have no intention of telling him we are going, have you? You are planning a moonlit flit, aren't you? I hate moonlit flits. You *always* do this to me."

"I don't always do this to you. I haven't done this to you since the Russian landlady."

The moonlit flit from the Russian landlady had been in Wellington. We'd been renting a house from a woman straight out of a Dostoevsky novel, the kind of woman who made pushing landladies down the stairs seem quite a reasonable thing to do. Her name was Irene and she was quite, quite mad.

She used to let herself into the house all the time. I'd come out of my room and there she'd be in the passage. And then she'd start shouting, because she'd spotted something she didn't like.

I was terrified of her. So when the time came to leave, I'd persuaded Polly the only way to do so without incurring unimaginably terrible Russian scenes, was to do a moonlit flit. So that's what we did. We left in the middle of the night by car with two cats. It was quite literally a moonlight flit, posting the keys on our way.

I was just as scared of Kyrie Z as I'd been of the Russian Landlady, and knew full well he was quite capable of making terrible Greek scenes.

"I'm scared of him," I said now to Polly. "I don't speak enough Greek to make him understand what's going on, and he will shout. You've seen how he shouts."

Kyrie Zacharias shouted a lot. And the trouble was, I never understood what he was shouting about. He was right up there with the Russian landlady, about as scary as they get. So I couldn't tell him we were going, I just couldn't.

"But how are we going to get away with it?" Polly wanted to know. "They are always there, they never go out."

And they were – they were always sitting on their balcony right above our front door, and they'd see the taxi come and they'd see Polly's iceberg of luggage, the suitcases, the boxes and the bags. And because they weren't stupid, they'd know at once we were doing a flit.

"I don't know," I said, "all I know is I'm not telling him."

Because she spoke only one word of Greek, ('kalimera'), something she was quite proud about, there was nothing at all she could do about it. It was a source of considerable frustration for her, because Polly wasn't nearly such a coward as I was, and she wasn't at all afraid of Kyrie Z and wouldn't have minded telling him at all.

By the time the morning of the great flit arrived, I was in a terrible state. I was having visions of Kyrie Z running down the street after us, shaking his fist; visions of Kyrie Z chasing our taxi in his pickup truck, forcing us off the road, and forcibly removing the suitcases from the taxi, before making us return. Most of all I was having visions of Kyrie Z shouting.

Please, I said to God. *I know I'm an appalling coward. I know this is morally wrong. I know I have no right to ask you to do anything to help. But please can you help anyway?*

"Look," cried Polly, from the window. "Look!" She'd come round to the idea of the moonlit flit in the end, because she had a strong streak of pragmatism and knew she had no choice. And besides, she was getting her way in the far larger matter of our exodus from Greece, and so the reprehensible manner of our parting was a small price to pay.

I looked out the window and saw to my amazed relief that Kyrie and Kyria Z were loading up their pickup truck with agricultural implements, presumably to do something agricultural in the olive grove they owned in the hills beyond. And this after not moving from their balcony for weeks. Next thing they were bucketing down the road, and disappearing from view.

"Quick," said Polly. "There's no time to waste. Go get the taxi now." And so I bolted up the road to the taxi rank and commandeered one. We loaded it up to the ceiling, Polly got in the front and I crammed myself into what little space was left on the back seat.

Then we waved goodbye to Methoni for the last time, Polly joyously, and I sadly, because after that, of course, no matter how much I might want to, I could not go back there. And that, of course, was the main disadvantage of moonlight flits, because they did tend to leave you with a whole lot of places you could never return to.

But on the positive side, if nothing else, the episode did confirm my belief that God is indeed compassionate towards the unworthy and the cowardly. And if you are reading this and feel any stirrings of self-righteousness and the temptation to judge (you know who you are), I have just one thing to say: *Let he or she who is without sin cast the first stone.*

The taxi drive to Kalamata was terrifying. I kept looking behind to see if Kyrie Z was pursuing us. He would have had a job catching us if so, because our taxi driver seemed determined to kill us first with his speed. But in my disturbed mind, Kyrie Z had developed superhuman powers, and I would have put nothing past him, and didn't even start to relax until we were safely aboard the coach to Athens.

I didn't get to relax for long. Polly wasn't happy about the coach. The rear, where we started out was too bumpy. The front, where we moved next, was too hot. The middle, where we went after that, was too crowded.

And then came the words every travelling companion dreads.

"I'm going to be sick. Tell the driver to stop."

"I can't," I said in anguish. "There's nowhere to stop. And even if there were somewhere, he won't." We were climbing one of those nightmarish winding mountain roads at the time and there was quite literally nowhere to stop.

"Do something," said Polly. "It's an emergency. If you don't do something I shall be sick."

So I fished out a packet of tissues, and a plastic bag, which I handed to her, and everything that happened immediately after that is a bit of a blur, which is probably a mercy.

Polly had a long history of earning the title Worst Travelling Companion in the World. I remember one incident when we were driving from Auckland to Wellington. I am not sure why we were doing so, that more significant detail is lost to memory. What isn't lost to memory is Polly announcing midway between Tikisomewhere and Tikisomewherelse that she needed the toilet, and she needed it now.

I tried to persuade her to hang on till Tikisomewherelse, but it was no good. "I shall have an accident if you don't find me a farmhouse," she said. "Hurry, it's an emergency."

Poor Polly had a problem with her bowels, along with all her other problems, and when she had to go, she had to go. So I was forced to turn off at the gate to some isolated farmhouse and, when I pulled out upside, go and knock on the door and ask the farmer if my mother could use their toilet…

There was another incident, a few years before that, that also sticks in my memory. My brother (the same brother who effectively brought an end to the Greek idyll by offering an unattractive alternative), was transporting Polly and me from one end of the country to the other. Again I forget the details of where we were going and why.

But what sticks in my mind is that Polly decided it was essential we take a dining table with us. A full-on six seater dining table, in a regular family-sized saloon car. It took up the whole of the car and poked my brother, who was driving, in the back of the neck all the way. I was crouched beneath it, on the back seat. My brother was furious, and said not a word for about 300 kilometers, before finally relenting, and starting to laugh.

It was a relief to get to Athens at last, but again a short-lived relief, for it turned out I'd managed to book us a hotel in the middle of the red-light district where all the gangsters hung out and that was probably why it had been so cheap.

I didn't even know Athens had a red light district, or gangsters, but apparently we were to bed down in the midst of them. Our taxi driver was very disapproving, and Polly, when she learned the reason for his disapproval, even more so. It didn't look any different from any other Athenian street, when we got there, so I left Polly to bewail our fate, and worry about gangsters, while I took on the red light district in search of something for our last supper.

I walked through the now-familiar Greek streets, in search of a suitable takeaway joint, reflecting that it would all soon be over. I was heading for a land of snow and call-centre jobs and tiresome older brothers who had somehow managed to get God on their side. But I'd had my mid-life crisis. It was well and truly over. I'd got it out of my system, I'd done the crazy thing that I needed to do in order to settle down to a life of filling hot water bottles and making cups of Tetley's tea.

The rest of the journey was filled with all the usual horribleness that characterized travels with Polly, mostly because she needed a fresh hot-water bottle for her back every half an hour, and it all ended with me in a foul mood swearing I'd never travel with her anywhere, ever, ever again.

But now, some years later, Polly has gone to a place where the marmalade is always perfect and the beaches are always the right colour, and I'd give my left arm to have to make her yet another hot water bottle, and travel with her wherever she wants to go, but it's too late.

I'm no longer in Scotland, having managed to end up in Wales, a land where the valleys are most assuredly green. There's somehow only one problem: it's the wrong shade of green.

Finis

Thank you for reading this book. If you enjoyed it, please take a moment to leave a review.

OTHER BOOKS BY MARGARET ELEANOR LEIGH

WITH REGRET

What if that Van Gogh hanging on the gallery wall is really a forgery?

Art historian Charlotte James is trying to put the past behind her, as well she might. That criminal conviction isn't anything to be proud of. So when a dodgy dealer called Evans comes tapping on her door, saying he's got some 'bits and pieces' that no doubt fell off the back of a museum van, her instinct is to walk away. But Charlotte isn't in a position to be fussy about clients. Her business is circling the plughole, and lately she's been reduced to cataloguing teapots. So she ignores the voice of reason and good sense and steps into Evans' world.

He's somehow got his hands on a drawing that appears to be a genuine Van Gogh. There's only one problem. The original is hanging on the walls of the Museum of Modern Art in Cardiff. Or is it?

Thus begins an investigation that will take Charlotte back to World War II, a time when London's major art collections were evacuated to the countryside to avoid the Blitz. It was also a time that afforded someone the perfect opportunity for a little light forgery.

In uncovering the crimes of the past, Charlotte must also confront the villains of the present, and this includes Evans. She has some assistance in the form of her grumbling, reluctant accomplice, Gareth, and while they might not be Holmes and Watson, they've certainly got their own unique chemistry

THE INCORRUPTIBLE

If you write anything about this, you will not leave Greece alive."

Trafficking in women is big business in Greece. Thousands of intended victims arrive in the country each year, unaware the respectable positions they've come to fill don't exist. What awaits them instead is a brutal initiation into a dark world from which few escape, and where mafia-style bosses ply their trade without let or hindrance.

So when Agnes Jones comes along, cycling round Greece with her tent, her primus and her high-flown ideals, it doesn't take long before she's made herself some powerful enemies.

The drama unfolds in a deceptively paradisiacal setting on the Peloponnesian peninsular. But Agnes Jones isn't quite what she seems either: she's not just a travelling journalist who has stumbled by accident into something dark and dirty.

A DEADLY DOCTRINE

When Patricia Temple dies suddenly, even the police assume suicide. After all, a theological college in New Zealand is the last place anyone expects foul play. Plenty of people disliked her, certainly, but surely no-one disliked her enough to break the First Commandment...

ABOUT MARGARET ELEANOR LEIGH

Margaret Eleanor Leigh is a writer without roots. Born and raised in apartheid South Africa, she's lived in Wales, New Zealand, England, Greece and Scotland. Now she's back in Wales, the land of her fathers. Her working past is just as colourful: she's been a journalist, a bureaucrat, a university tutor, a bookseller, and a proofreader.

This unsettled and chaotic life has its drawbacks. The only place she can honestly call home is the seat in front of her computer. But it also has its advantages: giving her a rich seam of experiences to mine — an invaluable resource for any writer.

.

You can connect with Margaret at
http://www.books.wordwinnower.com

Printed in Great Britain
by Amazon